The Happiest People on Earth

Further information about the Full Gospel Business Men's Fellowship International can be obtained from:

WORLD HEADQUARTERS: P.O. Box 5050, Costa Mesa, California 92626.

EUROPEAN OFFICE: Avenue Alfred Solvay, 1, 1170 Brussels, Belgium.

ASIAN OFFICE: Bible House, Suite 201, 7 Armenian Street, Singapore 6.

PACIFIC OFFICES: Australian National Office – P.O. Box 175, Nundah, Queensland, 4012, Brisbane.
New Zealand National Office – 139 Hurst Mere Road, Takapuna, Auckland.

AFRICAN OFFICE: Posbus/P.O. Box 196, Honeydew, Transvaal, South Africa.

The Happiest People on Earth

The long-awaited personal story of

Demos Shakarian

as told to

John and Elizabeth Sherrill

HODDER AND STOUGHTON

LONDON SYDNEY AUCKLAND TORONTO

Scripture quotations in this volume are from the King James Version of the Bible and from the Revised Standard Version of the Bible, copyrighted 1946, 1952 © 1971 and 1973.

Contents

Foreword

It was a grey December day in 1960 when we pulled our station wagon into the next to last parking place in front of the President Hotel in Atlantic City.

Seconds later a travel-worn Cadillac with California licence plates turned into the space beside us and out climbed a big man in a broad-brimmed Stetson. He stuck out a huge, work-scarred hand.

"I'm Demos Shakarian," he said.

He stepped around to the other side of his car and held the door for a pretty, dark-haired woman. "And this is my wife Rose."

We explained to them that we were reporters for *Guideposts* magazine assigned to investigate speaking in tongues, adding quickly that we were here "just to look."

We had quite a look. The President Hotel was the scene that week of a regional convention of an organisation called the Full Gospel Business Men's Fellowship International, of which Demos was the founder and president. Thousands had come to Atlantic City from all over the eastern seaboard, some to meet this same farm-tanned man in the Stetson hat, some to exchange stories about what the Holy Spirit was doing in their lives, and some, like us, just to look – a little fearfully and more than a little sceptically.

Watch out for emotionalism, we warned each other – shouting, arm-waving, frenzied testimonies – the time-worn techniques for whipping a large crowd into a state of excitement.

We watched ... and nothing of the sort occurred. From

the front of the hotel ballroom Demos conducted the meetings with the hushed sensitivity of one who listened for a
voice we could not hear. Instead of the chaos we expected, a
restrained and orderly joy governed the convention. Having
armoured ourselves against assaults that did not come, we
had no defence against the love we actually encountered and
that week we, along with hundreds of others, began our own
walk in the Spirit.

In the fifteen years since that December we have followed
the Pentecostal movement in many parts of the world,
because we've found this is where the good stories are – the
excitement, the changed lives, the reality in the church today.
And as we did we began to notice an interesting thing.
Wherever we talked to people whose faith was alive – men
and women, kids and old people, Roman Catholics and
Mennonites – time after time the story would begin with this
extraordinary group of businessmen, and a dairy farmer from
Downey, California named Demos Shakarian.

How was it possible, we kept asking ourselves, that this
shy, inarticulate man with the slow gentle smile, a man who
never seems to hurry, never seems to know today where he'll
be tomorrow, could be having such an impact on millions of
people? We decided to interview him to find out.

This was easier decided than done. Demos might be in
Boston or Bangkok or Berlin, and Demos doesn't answer his
mail. But over the past four years we've managed a number
of visits. Demos and Rose came east to see us; later we met
in a friend's chalet in Switzerland. We worked in Monaco
and Palm Springs. We talked in cars and airports and
Armenian restaurants. Best of all was the time we spent with
Demos and Rose at their home in Downey – the same small
house they built in 1934 when their first child was born.
Demos' father's house is next door, empty since his dad's
death. It's a lot grander place with a lot more room, but

Demos and Rose — well, there are certain memories in that smaller house.

And gradually we began to grasp Demos' secret.

Part of it his family brought with them from Armenia. This oldest Christian nation is also the one which has suffered most for its faith. And out of suffering has come insight.

But it's an insight bigger than any race or nation. It's a secret every one of us needs to know, for when we do, as Demos says, "no matter what the condition of the world around us, we will be the happiest people on earth."

November, 1975

John and Elizabeth Sherrill
Chosen Books
Lincoln, Virginia

1

The Message From Over the Mountain

The other night Rose and I were driving through Los Angeles on our way home, when suddenly I got a yearning to get off the freeway and drive past the house where my grandfather Demos lived when he first came to America.

After forty-two years of marriage Rose is used to these sudden impulses, so although it was one o'clock in the morning she said not a word as I turned down a ramp into the area that used to be called the Los Angeles Flats. The square stucco house was no longer standing at 919 Boston Street. We sat for a moment in the car, looking round us at the new federal housing which has replaced the rundown old neighbourhood. Then I turned the car around and headed back to the highway.

But with me, through the warm California night, travelled memories of Grandfather. I knew why I had needed to make this detour tonight: It was because of a prophecy Rose and I had heard earlier in the evening. We'd been at a Full Gospel Business Men's meeting in Beverly Hills where someone had made the prediction, claiming to be voicing God's own words, that a great persecution of Christians was soon to take place in many parts of the world, including the United States of America.

What were we to make of a statement like that? What had my family made of a similar message a century ago? For there had been such a prophecy then, too, and everything that had happened since in my grandfather's life and my father's life and my own had been the result of taking it seriously.

It was two A.M. when I turned into our driveway in Downey, a moonlit hour far too lovely for sleeping. I'm a late night person, much to Rose's despair – so she went on to bed while I pulled the old living-room chair close to the window, and sat there in the dark, letting my mind wander back into the past.

I never knew Grandfather Demos – he died before I was born – but I must have heard the stories about him a thousand times. I knew each detail so well that as I sat now looking out at the orange trees silvering in the moonlight, I seemed to be seeing another landscape, far away and long ago. This isn't hard for an Armenian. We're Old Testament people, the past and the present so woven together in our minds that what went on a hundred or a thousand or two thousand years ago is as real to us as the date on the calendar.

I'd heard it described so often that I could actually see the little village of Kara Kala sitting solidly in the rocky foothills of Mount Ararat – the mountain, so the Bible tells us, where Noah's ark came to rest. Closing my eyes I saw the stone building, the sheds and barns, and the one-room farm-house where my Grandfather Demos lived. In that house Grandfather's five daughters had been born – but no son – and that was a disgrace among the Armenians, as much a disgrace as it was among the ancient Israelites.

I could picture Grandfather walking to the house-church each Sunday morning with his five little girls. Although most Armenians were Orthodox, Grandfather

14

and many others in Kara Kala were Presbyterians. I could see him marching through the village to the house where church was meeting that particular Sunday, his head held high in the face of the silent reproach.

In view of his great need, it has always seemed surprising to me that Grandfather did not accept right away the strange message that had been trickling over the mountains for nearly fifty years. The message was brought by the Russians. Grandfather liked the Russians all right, he was just too levelheaded to accept their tales of miracles. The Russians came in long caravans of covered wagons. They were dressed as our people were, in long, high-collared tunics tied at the waist with tasselled cords, the married men in full beards. The Armenians had no difficulty understanding them as most of our people spoke Russian too. They listened to the tales of what the Russians called "the outpouring of the Holy Spirit" upon hundreds of thousands of Russian Orthodox Christians. The Russians came as people bringing gifts: the Gifts of the Spirit, which they wanted to share. I could just hear Grandfather and Grandmother talking late into the night after one of these visits. One had to admit, Grandfather would have said, that everything the Russians were talking about was Scriptural.

"I mean, healing is in the Bible. So is speaking in tongues. So is prophecy. It's just that the whole thing doesn't sound ... *Armenian*." By which he would have meant trustworthy. Down-to-earth. Practical.

And Grandmother, her heart forever heavy, might have said, "You know, when you talk about prophecy and healing, you're talking about miracles."

"Yes."

"If we were ever to 'receive the Holy Spirit' in this way, do you think *we* could ask for a miracle?"

"You mean like having a son?"

And then Grandmother might have started to cry. I know for a fact that on a certain sunny morning in May, 1891, Grandmother was weeping.

Over the years several families living in Kara Kala had begun to accept the message of the Russian Pentecostals. Grandfather's brother-in-law, Magardich Mushegan, was one of these. He received the Baptism of the Holy Spirit and on his frequent visits to the Shakarian farm would talk about the new-found joy in his life.

On this particular day – May 25, 1891 – Grandmother and several other women were sewing in a corner of the one-room farm house. That is, Grandmother was trying to sew, but tears kept falling on the material in her lap.

Across the room, next to the window where the light was good, Magardich Mushegan sat with his Bible open on his knee, reading.

Suddenly, Magardich snapped his Bible shut, got up and walked across the room. He stood in front of Grandmother, his heavy black beard bobbing up and down in his excitement.

"Goolisar," Magardich said. ". . . the Lord has just spoken to me!"

Grandmother's back straightened. "Yes, Magardich?"

"He's given me a message for you," Magardich said. "Goolisar, exactly one year from today, you will give birth to a son."

When Grandfather came in from the fields Grandmother met him at the door with the news of the wondrous prophecy. Pleased, wanting to believe yet still sceptical, Grandfather said nothing. He only smiled and shrugged his shoulders – and marked the date on the calendar.

The months passed and Grandmother became pregnant again. By this time everyone in Kara Kala knew of the prophecy, and the whole village waited in suspense. Then, on May 25, 1892, exactly a year from the day the prophecy was given, Grandmother gave birth to a baby boy.

It was the first time our family had encountered the Holy Spirit in this personal way. Everyone in Kara Kala agreed that the choice for the little boy's name was perfect: He was called *Isaac*, for he was, like Abraham's own long-awaited son, the child of promise.

I'm sure it was a proud and happy man who paraded his family to church each Sunday after Isaac was born. But Grandfather had a stubborn streak in him – all Armenians do. He considered himself too tough-minded to accept without reservation that he had witnessed a supernatural prophecy of the sort mentioned in the Bible. Maybe Magardich's prediction had been merely a lucky chance.

And then – all in one day – Grandfather's doubts disappeared once and for all.

In the year 1900, when Isaac was eight and his younger sister, Hamas, was four, the news arrived that a hundred Russian Christians were coming over the mountains in their covered wagons. Everyone was pleased. It was the custom in Kara Kala to hold a feast for the visiting Christians whenever they arrived. In spite of the fact that he didn't agree with the "full Gospel" preached by the Russians, Grandfather considered their visits as times set apart for God, and insisted that the welcoming feast be held on the large level plot of ground in front of his own home.

Now, Grandfather was proud of his fine cattle. With the news that the Russians were on their way, he went out to his herd and looked them over. He would choose the very finest, fattest steer for this special meal.

Unfortunately, however, the fattest steer in the herd turned out, on inspection, to have a flaw. The animal was blind in one eye.

What should he do? Grandfather knew his Bible well: He *knew* he should not offer an imperfect animal to the Lord, for didn't it say in the twenty-second chapter of Leviticus, verse 20, "But whatsoever hath a blemish, that shall ye not offer: for it shall not be acceptable . . ."?

What a dilemma! No other animal in the herd was large enough to feed a hundred guests. Grandfather looked around. No one was watching. Suppose he slaughtered the big steer and simply hid the blemished head? Yes, that was what he would do! Grandfather led the half-blind steer into the barn, butchered it himself, and quickly placed the head in a sack which he hid beneath a pile of threshed wheat in a dark corner.

Grandfather was just in time, for as he finished dressing the beef, he heard the rumble of wagons coming into Kara Kala. What a welcome sight! Coming down the dusty road was the familiar caravan of wagons, each pulled by four perspiring horses. Beside the driver of the first team, erect and commanding as ever, sat the white-bearded patriarch who was leader and prophet of the group. Grandfather and little Isaac ran up the road to greet their guests.

All over town preparations for the feast were underway. Soon the big steer was roasting on a spit over a huge bed of charcoal. That evening everyone gathered, expectant and hungry, around the long plank tables. Before the meal could begin, however, the food must be blessed.

These old Russian Christians would not say any prayer — even grace over meals — until they had received what they called *the anointing.* They would wait before the Lord until, in their phrase, the Spirit fell upon them. They claimed (a little to Grandfather's amusement), that they could literally *feel* His Presence descend. When this occurred they would raise their arms and dance with joy.

On this occasion as always, the Russians waited for the anointing of the Spirit. Sure enough, as everyone watched, first one and then another began to dance in place. Everything was going as usual. Soon would come the blessing of the food, and the feast could begin.

But to Grandfather's dismay, the patriarch suddenly raised his hand – not in sign of blessing – but as a signal that everything was to stop. Giving Grandfather a strange penetrating look, the tall white-haired man walked from the table without a word.

Grandfather's eyes followed the old man's every movement as the prophet strode across the yard and into the barn. After a moment he reappeared. In his hand he held the sack which Grandfather had hidden beneath the pile of wheat.

Grandfather began to shake. How could the man have known! No one had seen him. The Russians had not even reached the village when he had hidden that head. Now the patriarch placed the telltale sack before Grandfather and let it fall open, revealing to everyone the head with the milk-white eye.

"Have you anything to confess, Brother Demos?" the Russian asked.

"Yes, I have," said Grandfather, still shaking. "But how did you know?"

"God told me," the old man said simply. "You still do not believe that He speaks to His people today as in the past. The Spirit gave me this word of knowledge for a special reason: that you and your family might believe. You have been resisting the power of the Spirit. Today is the day you will resist no longer."

Before his neighbours and guests that evening Grandfather confessed the deception he had attempted. With tears rolling down his face into his bristly beard, he asked their forgiveness. "Show me," he said to the prophet, "how I, too, can receive the Spirit of God."

Grandfather knelt and the old Russian laid his work-gnarled hands on his head. Immediately Grandfather burst into joyous prayer in a language neither he nor anyone present could understand. The Russians called this kind of ecstatic utterance "tongues" and regarded it as a sign that the Holy Spirit was present with the speaker. That night Grandmother, too, received this "Baptism in the Spirit."

It was the beginning of great changes in our family's life, and one of the first was a change in attitude toward Kara Kala's most famous citizen. This person was known throughout the region as the "Boy Prophet" even though at the time of the incident with the steer's head the Boy Prophet was fifty-eight years old.

The man's real name was Efim Gerasemovitch Klubniken, and he had a remarkable history. He was of Russian origin, his family being among the first Pentecostals to come across the border, settling permanently in Kara Kala. From earliest childhood Efim had shown a gift for prayer, frequently going on long fasts, praying around the clock.

As everybody in Kara Kala knew, when Efim was eleven years old he had heard the Lord calling him again to one of his prayer vigils. This time he persisted for seven days and nights, and during this time received a vision.

This in itself was not extraordinary. Indeed, as Grandfather had been accustomed to grumble, anyone who went that long without eating or sleeping was bound to start seeing things. But what Efim was able to *do* during those seven days was not so easy to explain.

Efim could neither read nor write. Yet, as he sat in the little stone cottage in Kara Kala, he saw before him a vision of charts and a message in a beautiful handwriting. Efim asked for pen and paper. And for seven days sitting at the rough plank-table where the family ate, he laboriously copied down the form and shape of letters and diagrams that passed before his eyes.

When he had finished, the manuscript was taken to people in the village who could read. It turned out that this illiterate child had written out in Russian characters a series of instructions and warnings. At some unspecified time in the future, the boy wrote, every Christian in Kara Kala would be in terrible danger. He foretold a time of unspeakable tragedy for the entire area, when hundreds of thousands of men, women, and children would be brutally murdered. The time would come, he warned, when everyone in the region must flee. They must go to a land across the sea. Although he had never seen a geography book, the Boy Prophet drew a map showing exactly where the fleeing Christians were to go. To the amazement of the adults, the body of water depicted so accurately in the drawing was not the nearby Black Sea, or the Caspian Sea, or even the farther-off Mediterranean, but the distant and unimaginable Atlantic Ocean! There was no doubt about it, nor about the identity of the land on the other side: the map plainly indicated the east coast of the United States of America.

But the refugees were not to settle down there, the prophecy continued. They were to continue travelling until they reached the west coast of the new land. There, the boy wrote, God would bless them and prosper them, and cause their seed to be a blessing to the nations.

A little later Efim also wrote out a second prophecy, but all anybody knew about that one was that it dealt with the still more distant future – when the people would once again have to flee. Efim asked his parents to seal this prophecy in an envelope, and repeated the instructions he had received concerning it. He had been told in his vision that only a future prophet – chosen by the Lord for this task – could open the envelope and read the prophecy to the church. Anyone opening the envelope before this time would die.

Well, many people in Kara Kala smiled at these romances

of a little boy. Surely there must be some explanation of the "miraculous" writing. Perhaps he had secretly taught himself to read and write, just in order to play this trick on the village.

Others however took to calling Efim the Boy Prophet and were not at all convinced that the message was not genuine. Every time news of fresh political troubles reached the tranquil hills around Ararat, they would get out the now-yellowed pages and read them again. Troubles between the Moslem Turks and the Christian Armenians did seem to be growing in intensity. In August, 1896 – four years before Grandfather butchered the blind steer – hadn't a Turkish mob murdered more than six thousand Armenians on the streets of Constantinople?

But Constantinople was far away, and years had passed since the giving of the prophecy. True, prophecies in the Bible often came dozens, even hundreds of years before the event. But most people in Kara Kala, Grandfather among them, believed such genuine prophetic gifts had ceased with the completion of the Bible.

And then, a little after the turn of the century, Efim announced that the time was near for the fulfilment of the words he had written down nearly fifty years before. "We must flee to America. All who remain here will perish."

Here and there in Kara Kala Pentecostal families packed up and left the holdings that had been their ancestral possessions time out of mind. Efim and his family were among the first to go. As each group of Pentecostals left Armenia, they were jeered by those who remained behind. Sceptical and disbelieving folk – including many Christians – refused to believe that God could issue pinpoint instructions for modern people in a modern age.

But the instructions proved correct. In 1914 a period of unimaginable horror arrived for Armenia. With remorseless efficiency the Turks began the bloody business of driving two-thirds of the population out into the Mesopotamian desert. Over a million men, women and children died in these marches, including every inhabitant of Kara Kala. Another half a million were massacred in their villages, in a pogrom that was later to provide Hitler his blueprint for the extermination of the Jews. "The world did not intervene when Turkey wiped out the Armenians," he reminded his followers. "It will not intervene now."

The few Armenians who managed to escape the besieged areas brought with them tales of great heroism. They reported that the Turks sometimes gave Christians an opportunity to deny their faith in exchange for their lives. The favourite procedure was to lock a group of Christians in a barn and set it afire: "If you are willing to accept Mohammed in place of Christ we'll open the doors." Time and again, the Christians chose to die, chanting hymns of praise as the flames engulfed them.

Those who had heeded the warning of the Boy Prophet and sought asylum in America, heard the news with dismay.

Grandfather Demos was among these who had fled. After his experience with the Russian patriarch, Grandfather no longer discounted the validity of prophecy. In 1905 he sold the farm which had been in the family for generations, accepting whatever bit of money he could get for it. Then he selected the possessions that his family would carry on their backs, including in his own load the heavy wood-burning brass samovar. And with his wife, his six daughters, Shushan, Esther, Siroon, Magga, Yerchan, and Hamas, and the pride of his life, thirteen-year-old Isaac, he set out for America.

The family reached New York safely but, mindful of the prophecy, did not settle there. In accordance with the written

23

instructions they kept travelling across the vast bewildering new land, until they reached Los Angeles. There, to their delight, they found a small but growing Armenian sector where several friends from Kara Kala were already living. With the help of these friends Grandfather went househunting. "The Flats" was the cheapest section of Los Angeles; even so it was only by joining together with two other newly arrived families that he was able to move his family into the square-shaped stucco house at 919 Boston Street.

The ship passage, the trip across the United States, and his share of the new home had taken all the money from the sale of the ancestral farm, and Grandfather set out at once to look for work. Without success. The great depression of the late 1800s was still being felt in California: there were no jobs to be had, especially for a newcomer who spoke not a word of the language. Every morning Grandfather would go down to the hiring halls, and every evening he would return with his step a little heavier than the day before.

But there was one time each week when all cares were set aside: the Sunday worship service. The house in Boston Street had a large front parlour which quickly became the community meeting place. The service followed the customs of the house churches back in Kara Kala. The focal point was a large table on which lay an open Bible. On either side of the room, just as it had always been, were the women, also seated according to age. The elders continued to sport full black beards, although occasionally a younger man shocked everybody by growing only a moustache. And it was expected that, for church (if not for the rest of the week), the men would wear their bright-hued tunics, the women the long, embroidered dresses and hand-crocheted head scarves that had come down through the generations.

What comfort it must have given Grandfather to draw on spiritual support from this body of Christians. They had long

since learned that God could speak to them directly from the
Bible. With his need for work on his mind, Grandfather
would kneel on the small oriental rug that had been brought
from the old country and ask "for a word." Then the whole
congregation would start to pray softly, often in the unknown, ecstatic languages called tongues. At last one of the
elders would step to the Bible and place his finger on a passage at random. Always the words seemed to speak straight
to the need. Maybe they were about the Lord's faithfulness,
or about the coming of milk-and-honey days just as the Boy
Prophet had foretold. Well, the little Armenian church was
waiting for those days to arrive, but at least while it waited,
there were these beautiful moments of communion.

One day there was another encouragement. It happened
that Grandfather and his brother-in-law, Magardich
Mushegan (the same man who had predicted Isaac's birth)
were walking down San Pedro Street in Los Angeles, looking
for work in the livery stables. As they passed a side road
called Azusa Street they stopped short. Along with the smell
of horses and harness leather came the unmistakable sounds
of people praising God in tongues. They had not known that
anywhere in the United States were people who worshipped
as they did. They rushed up to the converted stable from
which the sounds were coming and knocked on the door. By
now Grandfather had collected a few English words.

"Can we . . . in?" Grandfather asked.

"Of course!" The door was flung open. There were
embraces, hands lifted to God in thanksgiving, singing, and
praising the Lord, and Grandfather and Magardich returned
to Boston Street with the news that Pentecost had come even
to this distant land across the sea. No one knew then that
Azusa Street was to become a famous name. There was a
revival going on in the old livery stable which would spark the
charismatic renewal in scores of different places around the

globe. At the moment Grandfather saw this other body of believers simply as a welcome confirmation of God's promise to do something new and wonderful in California.

What this new thing was, he did not live to see. The long-awaited steady job, when finally it came, ended in tragedy.

One day in 1906 Grandfather came home with a lilt to his walk.

"You've found work," Grandmother said.

"I have."

The entire household gathered around while Grandfather told the great news. Up in Nevada – that was another state, he explained, adjoining California – the railroads were hiring men.

Grandmother's face lost its smile. She had heard of Nevada. It was a desert where temperatures reached 120° and men fell dead as they tried to do the heavy work of track laying in that heat.

"But you forget," Grandfather countered, "I am a farmer. I'm used to working outside in the sun. Besides, Goolisar, mother of my son, have we a choice?"

So Grandfather called the elders of the church together and received from them the traditional blessing before a trip. Then with a change of clothes rolled in a blanket he headed off for the desert. Soon the mailman was delivering a postal money order each week to the house on Boston Street.

And then one summer evening came the wire Grandmother had always feared. On a blast-furnace day Grandfather had collapsed while working on the line. His body would be shipped back by train.

And with Grandfather's death my own father, Isaac, came into the job he was not ready for – at 14 he was now head of the family.

For several months Dad had been selling newspapers on

a street corner in downtown L.A. He earned nearly ten dollars a month which was a valuable contribution while Grandfather was alive but hardly enough to feed his mother and six sisters. Even such great journalistic moments as the San Francisco earthquake of 1906, when he sold six bundles of *Extras* inside an hour, did little more than put a few extra quarts of milk on the table.

Nor would Dad take money he had not worked for. In those early years of the century, gold coins were still in circulation – the five-dollar gold piece approximately the same size as the nickel. One day a customer hurriedly shoved a coin into Dad's hand, accepted three pennies change, and dashed off down the street. Dad was about to slip the coin into his blue newsboy's apron with the words LOS ANGELES TIMES printed across the front, when he glanced down and saw that the "nickel" he was holding was a five-dollar piece.

"Mister!" Dad shouted. But the customer was already a block away. Dad threw a weight on his papers and started after the man. A streetcar jangled past. Without thinking twice Dad jumped aboard, paid the fare out of his own precious earnings, and followed the man. When finally he caught up with him, Dad jumped off the trolley.

"Mister!" The man at last turned around. "Mister, this not nickel?" Dad said in his halting English. Dad held out his hand and the gold coin glinted in the sun.

I often think about that man, who took his money back with the merest grunt of acknowledgement. I like to think that if he could have seen the hungry faces waiting each night at the door of 919 Boston Street, he would have told the newsboy to keep it all.

Ten dollars a month was not enough for the family. In the evenings after work Dad began making the rounds of the hiring halls, just as his father had done before him. But if work for men was scarce, jobs for boys were fewer still.

At last he learned of an opening in a harness factory. The pay was low — fifteen dollars a month — but even so it was more than he could earn selling papers, and Dad took the job.

One day in 1908, when Dad was sixteen, he came home from the factory to hear startling words from Grandmother.

"Isaac, such wonderful news!" Grandmother said.

"We can use some," Dad answered through the handkerchief he often held to his mouth. The fine leather dust at the harness factory got into his lungs and caused a continual cough.

"I've got a job!" Grandmother said.

Dad couldn't believe he had heard right. No Armenian woman worked for a wage. In the old country, men provided for their families, he reminded Grandmother out in the kitchen as he washed the leather dust from his hair.

"But Isaac, can't you see what carrying this burden alone is doing to you? You're thin as the skewer in a kebab. I even heard you speak sharply to Hamas yesterday."

Dad blushed but held his ground. "You are not going to take work."

"I already have. A nice family in Hollenbeck Park. Washing, ironing, just a little cleaning."

"Then I'll go pack," Dad said softly and left the kitchen.

He went up to his own room, Grandmother following. She stood in the door as he rolled his few clothes into a bundle. "With you working, you won't need me here any more."

The next day Grandmother informed the people in Hollenbeck Park that she would not be coming to do their laundry after all.

But at the harness factory Dad's cough grew worse. It did not improve, even when he was made foreman the following year and could occasionally be off the floor. Grandmother used to tell me how she would lie awake listening to Dad cough his way through the night. When she finally persuaded him to see a doctor, the physician confirmed what everybody in the family already knew: If Dad didn't quit the harness factory, he would not live out his teens.

The question was: How else could he support his mother and sisters? And here, as the family always did in times of perplexity, Dad turned to the church.

The Armenian Pentecostals no longer worshipped in the parlour of the house on Boston Street. As the men had found work here and there, the first thing they did was to construct a church building. It was a small frame structure on Gless Street, perhaps sixty feet by thirty, with backless benches that could be shoved against the wall when the joy of the Lord moved the congregation to dance in the Spirit. At the front end of the room was the traditional Table.

I can picture Dad walking up to the Table just as his father had done on so many occasions. He knelt on the little dark maroon rug and stated his need, while behind him grouped the elders, including Magardich and Magardich's son Aram Mushegan who, it was said, was so strong he could lift a wagon clear off the ground while you repaired a wheel. It was Aram who placed his finger on the Bible now and read aloud strange and beautiful words:

Blessed shall you be in the city, and blessed shall you be in the field. Blessed shall be the fruit of your body, and the fruit of your ground, and the fruit of your beasts, the increase of your cattle . . .

Ground? Dad wondered. Cattle? But the wonderful words from the 28th chapter of Deuteronomy continued:

*The Lord will command the blessing upon you in your
barns, and in all that you undertake; and he will bless
you in the land which the Lord your God gives you.*

And as he listened Dad realised that there was only one
thing in the world he'd ever really wanted to do – the thing
he dreamed of all day over the cutting machines. He
wanted to work with cows and fresh, green, growing things in
the out of doors.

But it takes a lot of money to buy land, he'd reminded
himself whenever his thoughts had reached this point. Now,
with the promise of Scripture ringing in his ears, he made up
his mind. Dad gave notice at the harness factory, and
within two weeks was without a job.

And almost at once he began to notice something. The
fruits and vegetables displayed in the stores around the city
were not only priced too high for families like his to afford,
they were often small and pale-looking, as though they'd
been picked green. What would happen, he wondered, if he
were to pick up really fresh vegetables from the country and
bring them into town to sell, house to house?

And so it was that Dad launched his produce business.
South and east of Los Angeles was an area of small farms,
many of them owned by Armenians, where some of the
choicest fruits and vegetables in the world were raised.
Dad took the bit of money he had been setting aside month
by month toward his sisters' dowries, and with it made
two purchases. He bought a flatbed wagon. And he bought
a two-year-old, rust-coloured horse named Jack.

The next day Dad drove Jack and his wagon out to a little
railroad junction called Downey, in those days not a suburb
of the city, but a small town fifteen miles in the country. The
trip took the better part of three hours each way, but Dad
loved every minute of it. The clean fresh air flooded his

threatened lungs with healing. In Dad's mind the dream was beginning to grow: One day he too would be a farmer. He would even own cows. He'd be a dairyman — the best dairyman in the country.

But meanwhile there was work to do. That day in Downey Dad went from farm to farm picking up lettuce here, grapefruit and oranges there, carrots somewhere else — whatever fruits and vegetables were in peak season. Then, his wagon heaped with the prime produce, he drove back into Los Angeles. As Jack clip-clopped up and down the streets of the city, Dad called his wares: "Ripe strawberries! Sweet oranges! Fresh-picked spinach!" His produce was good, his prices fair, and the next time he came by he found that housewives were waiting for him.

Another year passed. Dad was now nineteen, sporting a stylish moustache. The dowry money had been replaced with more added to it. With his health returned and his business flourishing, Dad considered that it was time to begin thinking of a family of his own.

Already he had spotted the girl he would like to have for his wife, a black-eyed, black-haired fifteen-year-old named Zarouhi Yessayian. Not that he knew Zarouhi personally. According to Armenian custom, no boy and girl might speak to one another until after their families had agreed upon marriage. Dad knew only that when he passed the Yessayian house at Sixth and Gless Street his heart turned over in his chest.

Since Dad's father was dead, an elder at the church made the formal request for Zarouhi's hand. To the Yessayians he described Dad's prospects: Just as soon as he had saved up enough for the down payment, he was going to sell his produce business and buy dairy land. After that, the young man claimed, the very skies of California themselves were his only limit.

So Dad married. Soon, he and my mother were able to buy ten acres of cornfields, eucalyptus trees, and pasture land in the heart of Downey. And most wonderful of all — three milk cows. With their own hands, he and Mother built a little house of unfinished plankwood. Mother used to say it was an easy house to clean — the twelve-inch floorboards were so loose fitting that the scrub water simply ran through the cracks onto the ground beneath.

With a start I realised that, as I sat reminiscing in the old livingroom chair, the sky had grown pale behind the orange trees. And still my thoughts lingered in the past. On July 21, 1913, even before Dad and Mother finished the little plank house in Downey, their first child was born. Unlike Grandfather who had waited so long for a son, Mother and Dad's first baby was a boy. They called me Demos.

On the table beside me the big brass samovar, which Grandfather carried on his back from Kara Kala, was catching the early light. I turned to look at it, its well-rubbed sides glowing gold in the dawn. And I wondered if in naming me after Grandfather, my parents guessed the mysterious and far-reaching role prophecy was to play in my life as well.

2

Union Pacific Avenue

Although my parents moved to Downey when I was eight months old, they continued to attend the little church on Gless Street. Dad said it was from their churches that Armenians drew their strength. Dad taught me two skills at about the same time. As soon as my hands were big enough, he taught me how to milk. And as soon as I was tall enough to stand on an orange crate and reach Jack's head he showed me how to harness up. Some of my earliest memories are of hitching Jack to the buggy and setting out with the family — by now I had two sisters, Ruth and Lucy — for church.

The trip still took three hours each way, and the service with the midday meal lasted five, and I enjoyed every bit of it. I liked to watch those muscular farmers and day-labourers thrusting their hands into the air as the Spirit swept the meeting, faces raised heavenward until their long black beards pointed straight out, parallel to the top of the Table. I loved to hear their deep rich voices chanting the ancient Armenian psalter.

Even the sermons were enthralling, because then the past sprang to life there in the little frame building on Gless Street. Armenia, the preacher would remind us, is the oldest

Christian nation in the world, and also the one which has suffered most for her faith. The recent Turkish massacres were only the latest in the record of savage attempts by her neighbours to annihilate the small stubborn country – and by constant retelling our history became bone and fibre of us all.

"It is the year 287," the preacher would begin, "and young Saint Gregory is wondering if he dares return home to his beloved Armenia." Gregory had fallen out of favour with the king and been exiled from the country, but in exile he has heard the Christian message. At last in spite of the risk he decides to come back to share the gospel with his countrymen.

The king soon learns of his return, has him seized and thrown into the deepest dungeon of the castle to die of starvation. But not before the king's sister had listened to Gregory's preaching and become a believer. The preacher would paint a vivid picture of the young woman stealing down dank stone stairs to the black, foul-smelling dungeon, hiding a loaf of bread or a gourd of goat's milk beneath her rippling cloak. For fourteen years she manages to keep the saint alive.

At that point a dreadful malady seizes the king, a strange insanity that hurls him to the floor grunting like an animal. During his lucid moments he beseeches his physicians to heal him, but no one can.

"The man named Gregory could help you," his sister suggests.

"Gregory died many years ago, " the king retorts. "His bones are rotting beneath this very castle."

"He is alive," she says softly, and describes her fourteen-year vigil.

So Gregory is brought from the dungeon, his hair as white as the snow on Mt. Ararat, but sound in mind and spirit. In the name of Jesus Christ, he rebukes the demon

34

tormenting the king, and in that instant the king is healed. Together, in the year 301, he and St. Gregory set out to achieve the conversion of all Armenia.

On the long ride home I would relive the story again, the patient man in the dark dungeon, locked away as year follows year, never losing faith, never losing hope, waiting only for God's perfect time. . . .

When the last of her six daughters married, Grandmother came to live with us in the little plank house. I remember her well, a tiny white-haired woman whose dark eyes shone with pride in her only son. Her only regret, she used to say, was that Grandfather Demos had not lived to see the Shakarians back again on land of their own. Goolisar died there in that little cabin, a happy and fulfilled woman.

Already, by the time I was ten, the dairy was prospering. The three cows had become thirty, then a hundred, then five hundred, and the original ten acres had grown to two hundred. Dad dreamed now of owning the largest and finest dairy farm in California. If work was what it took to do that, then it might just happen, too, for Dad knew how to work, and to see that the rest of us worked, too.

Besides myself there was now a bunkhouse full of Mexican-Americans working alongside us in the barns, and Dad and I had learned to speak Spanish. I don't know who enjoyed the other's stories more: their tales about Mexico or Dad's recollections of life in Armenia. They couldn't hear often enough about Efim the Boy Prophet, or how Magardich Mushegan had foretold Dad's birth. Every time a new hand joined us Dad had to tell the stories all over again.

Afterwards he'd always have to describe Efim's funeral in 1915, the largest one the Los Angeles Flats had ever seen. Efim had not attended the Gless Street church (where the services were in Armenian) but the Russian-language church a few blocks away. On the date of the great funeral, not only those two congregations joined together, but even Orthodox Armenians and Russians swallowed their objections to "wild Pentecostal goings-on" and attended the service, for many of them too had come to America as a result of his prophecy.

"And what about the second prophecy?" the Mexican-Americans would ask. "The one that's still to happen?"

"It's still being safeguarded. Efim's sons have it."

"And you die if you open it?"

"Unless you are the one appointed by the Lord."

"Who do you think that's going to be?"

But of course no one knew the answer to that. . . .

It was about the time of the Boy Prophet's death that I got the injury which was to cause me so many problems.

I never even knew how I broke my nose. A ten-year-old boy working around a farm gets a good many bumps. In any case, when I began to notice that I wasn't hearing as well as the other kids in the fifth grade, Mother took me to the doctor.

"I can tell you what the trouble is, Zarouhi," the doctor said, "but not what to do about it. Demos has broken his nose and it's healed wrong. Both the nasal passage and the ear canals are blocked. We can try an operation, but they aren't usually too successful."

And they weren't successful in my case either. Every year, it seemed, I went into the hospital for another operation, and every year the ear canals closed up again. In school I had to sit in the very first row in order to hear the teacher at all.

Although I never knew a time when Jesus wasn't a close friend, during these months when my deafness was growing worse, He seemed closer than ever. I could no longer take part in the team games the other boys played after school.

("Don't choose Demos. He can't hear too good.") So I was alone a lot. I didn't especially mind. My favourite chore on the farm was to weed the corn because then I could go far in the fields and talk to the Lord out loud. The summers when I was twelve and thirteen the long dim aisles seemed to me like a green cathedral, the great veined leaves arching overhead. There I would lift my hands in the air the way the men did at church:

"Let me hear again, Jesus! don't listen to what that doctor says about not getting better. . . ."

How well I remember every detail of that Sunday in 1926, when I was thirteen. I recall getting up and dressing in my room on the second floor of our new home. Dad had a thousand head of milk cows now, and had built a two-storey Spanish-style house with white stucco walls and a red-tile roof.

I felt funny as I dressed for church. Funny in a nice way, as if my whole body were in some sort of special spiritual tune. I went down the long curved staircase to breakfast singing. My parents and sisters were already at the table: by now three more little girls had joined the family. The youngest, Florence, was still a baby of two, but the four older girls were chattering excitedly about our weekly trip to town. I tried to join in but soon gave up. How could you talk to people who mumbled?

Our old horse, Jack, no longer pulled the family buggy fifteen miles into church each Sunday. The year before, when Jack reached sixteen, Dad had put him out to pasture to spend the rest of his life in well-deserved retirement. In his place we now had a long black Studebaker touring car with a canvas top and a box of spare axles beneath the back seat for the uneven farm roads.

That Sunday the little church hummed with excitement.

There was not a person in the room who did not remember what had happened *last* week. The mother of one of the women in the congregation had left Armenia two months before to join her daughter in America. There had been no word from her since, and the daughter was frantic. As the church had begun to pray about the situation, Aunt Esther's husband, Uncle George Stepanian, suddenly got up and strode to the door. For a long time he stood staring up the street as though seeing far horizons. At last he spoke. "Your mother is fine," he said. "She will be in Los Angeles in three days."

Three days later, the old lady arrived.

And so today the sense of expectancy was high, each one wondering what form the Lord's next blessing would take. Perhaps someone would be healed. Perhaps someone would receive guidance. . . .

Even as I was thinking this a strange thing began to happen — not to someone else, but to me. As I sat there on a rear bench with the other boys, I felt something like a heavy woollen blanket settle over my shoulders. I looked around, startled, but no one had touched me. I tried to move my arms, but they met resistance, like I was pulling them through water.

Suddenly my jaw began to shake as if I were shivering with cold, although the "blanket" felt warm. The muscles in the back of my throat tightened. I had a sudden yearning to tell Jesus that I loved Him, but when I opened my mouth to say so, out came words I couldn't understand. I knew they weren't Armenian, or Spanish, or English, but they poured out of me as though I'd been speaking them all my life. I turned to the boy next to me and he was all grins.

"Demos's got the Spirit!" he shouted, and all over the church people turned. Someone asked me a question, but though I understood him perfectly I could answer only in the bubbling, joyous new sounds. The whole church began to sing and praise God in delight, while I worshipped the Lord in my new language.

Even hours later, driving home in the car, anyone who spoke to me was answered in tongues. I went upstairs to my room and closed the door, and still the ecstatic unintelligible syllables spilled out of me. I put on my pyjamas and turned out the light. And at that moment the sense of the Lord's presence came over me more strongly than ever. It was as if the invisible mantle which had remained on my shoulders all evening had become irresistibly heavy – though not unpleasantly so. I sank to the floor and lay there on the rug absolutely helpless, unable to get up and get into bed. It was not a frightening experience, but a wholesome and refreshing one – like the special moment just before you fall into a deep sleep.

As I lay there in my room, time took on an eternal quality. And in that eternity I heard a voice. It was one I recognized very well indeed, for I had heard it often in my green cathedral out in the cornfields.

Demos, can you sit up? it asked.

I tried. But it was useless. Some incredibly strong, yet infinitely gentle power held me where I was. I knew that I was a strong boy – not as strong as Aram Mushegan, but very tough indeed for a thirteen-year-old. Yet my muscles had no more strength than a new-born calf's.

The voice was speaking again. *Demos, will you ever doubt My power?*

"No, Lord Jesus."

Three times the question was repeated. Three times I answered it.

Then all at once the power which had been all around me seemed to be inside as well. I felt a surge of superhuman energy – as if I could float right out of the house and sail the heavens in the power of God. I felt as if I could look down on earth from God's perspective, see all human need from the vantage point of His supply. And all the while He was whispering to my heart, *Demos, power is the birthright of every Christian. Accept power, Demos.*

And suddenly it was dawn. I could hear the mockingbirds outside my window.

I sat up with a start. I could hear *what?* It had been years since I had heard a bird singing.

I jumped to my feet, feeling wonderfully whole and alive, and scrambled into my clothes. It was after five A.M. and Dad and I had to be in the milking barns by five-thirty. As I opened my door that marvellous morning, I could hear the eggs sizzling down in the kitchen.

The click of dishes, the songs of birds, the clatter of my own feet as I raced down the red-tile staircase – these were the little sounds I had not realized I was missing. I burst into the kitchen, "Dad! Mother! I can hear!"

The healing was never total. When Mother and I returned to the doctor he discovered 90 per cent of normal hearing. Why I was left with the 10 per cent impairment I don't know, and I don't worry about it. I remember, later that same Monday morning when the milking was finished, going alone to my green cathedral. The corn was high, ready for harvest. I sat down between two rows, snapped off an ear, shucked it and nibbled at the white grains popping with milk. "Lord," I said, "I know that when You heal people it's because You have work for them to do.

"Will You show me, Lord, the job You have for me?"

At first – as the other boys in my class dreamed of becoming baseball stars – I dreamed of becoming a prophet. I was after all just a little older than the Boy Prophet had been when he had his vision.

But the years passed and I did not receive this wonderful gift. *Prophecy will play a large part in your life*, the Lord seemed to be saying, *but you will not be the prophet.*

Then one day I had an experience which made me wonder whether I was to become a healer. My youngest sister Florence was six years old when she fell against a stanchion pipe out in the barn and shattered her right elbow. By the time the surgeon and the bone specialist had finished their work they were confident that Florence would retain the use of her hand. But the elbow would forever remain bent and rigid. "When the cast comes off we can begin therapy. With patience she may regain ten, even twenty per cent articulation, but that's the best we can hope for."

One Sunday in church soon after this report, I felt again the sensation of a warm, heavy blanket settling over my shoulders. I did not need to ask Who it was, nor did I question what I should do: I was to step across the room and pray for the healing of Florence's arm.

So while everyone was singing a hymn, I got quietly up from my bench and walked over to the women's section. I leaned down to Florence, sitting on the last bench, her right arm encased in a huge plaster cast. The warmth of the blanket spread down my arms and into my hands.

"Florence," I whispered, "I'm going to pray for your elbow."

Her large black eyes regarded me solemnly. I placed my hands on the cast. Actually, I hardly prayed at all, but just stood there feeling the fire flood down my arms and hands into the plaster around Florence's elbow.

"I feel that!" Florence whispered. "It feels hot."

And that was all. In a moment the sensation of the mantle left me and I returned to my seat. I doubt if half a dozen people had noticed us.

A few weeks later the cast came off. At dinner that evening

Mother told us how the specialist had put one hand on the white, creased skin of Florence's elbow, taken her wrist with the other, and gingerly attempted to straighten the injured arm an inch or two. As the forearm swung all the way back, then forward, then in wide circles from the elbow, his face broke into an incredulous smile. "Well ... !" he kept saying. "Well! Better than I expected. Much better! Why, it's ... it's like an arm that never was broken!"

And so, out in the cornfield that summer, I found myself asking the Lord if healing was His work for me. Again I seemed to get an answer: *Of course. I want all My church to do this work. You'll see many wonderful healings, some through your own hands. But Demos, this is not My special work for you either.*

I was seventeen and a sophomore in high school – I should have been a senior, but I had lost two years because of my deafness – when Dad bought a second farm. We had room now to erect our own silos, and enough capital to install automatic-milking machines. He was getting into other businesses as well. A big headache for us and our neighbouring dairy farmers had always been getting our milk from farm to bottling plant. So Dad started a milk haulage business. Then, noting that the price of ham was up in L.A., Dad also got into hog raising. And then into meat packing. "The Lord will command the blessing upon you in all that you undertake. ..." It seemed indeed that everything Isaac, son of promise, touched was destined to thrive.

His success was all the more remarkable because these were the depression years of the early 'thirties. By now Dad had given me my own small herd to manage, and I remember the teacher who helped me set up bookkeeping records informing me wistfully that I was making more with my thirty cows than most of the teachers at Downey High.

To our home now gravitated politicians, businessmen, community leaders – and my mother, the shy little immigrant girl from Armenia, found herself hostessing weekly dinner parties for the powerful and prominent. She was a truly marvellous cook and soon her *dolmas, kuftas* and *katahs* were famous all over Southern California.

But what I chiefly remember about Mother's cooking was that she took the same pains no matter who the guest. Tramps were frequent callers in those days, and they got the same treatment as the mayor of Downey: the best china, the silver knives and forks, a cloth on the table. If no hot meal was ready, she would prepare one – meat, vegetables, home-made pastry – all the while urging the man in her limited English, "Sit! Sit! No hurry for eat!"

And meanwhile I found myself drawn more and more often to another address. Whenever business for the farm took me to East Los Angeles, I would find an excuse to wander past Sirakan Gabrielian's rambling cream-coloured home at 4311 Union Pacific Avenue, in the hopes that his daughter might suddenly appear in the yard. Not that I could have spoken to her if she had; boy-girl conversations – unless the two were engaged – were still unheard of in the Armenian community. But just knowing that she was close by filled me with an indescribable happiness.

And always there was Sunday to look forward to – Sunday when Rose Gabrielian would be sitting with the other girls on the women's side of the church – the prettiest girl in the room, the one all the boys surreptitiously followed with their eyes.

Her father's first name, Sirakan, meant *Sweetheart* in Armenian; I liked that. Like my own father, Sirakan Gabrielian had started out with nothing. Eventually he had scraped together one hundred dollars and – also like Dad – bought a horse and wagon. Sirakan, however, instead of hauling fruits and vegetables with his rig, went into the trash business. It was a much-needed service in Los Angeles just after the turn of the century, and soon he was able to buy a second horse and cart, then a third.

Sirakan and his family were Armenian Orthodox. He lived near the Gless Street church, however, and hearing the joyous sounds which poured from the open windows week after week, he decided to investigate. Before long he joined the congregation. And very nearly lost his life. To many Orthodox Armenians, the Pentecostals seemed like traitors to the ancient faith. To see one of their own join this hated group was the same as seeing him dead.

So they decided to bury him.

One day when Sirakan pulled up to the city dump with his load of refuse a gang of Orthodox believers was waiting for him. They pinioned his arms and legs and carried him to a pit they had dug in the sandy soil. They had thrown him into it and actually had several feet of dirt on top of him when a wagon driven by Pentecostals arrived, and in the free-for-all which followed Sirakan scrambled out.

I loved to hear him tell that story. I also liked to hear him tell about his marriage. When Sirakan was twenty-one his father had decided to return to Armenia in search of a wife, Sirakan's mother having died some years before. Sirakan's trash business was thriving by then, so he asked his father to bring back a bride for him as well.

Sirakan's father was successful in both quests. For his son he chose a pretty thirteen-year-old named Tiroon Marderosian. To facilitate her entry into the United States she was married by proxy there in Armenia, then set out on the long journey to join the husband she had never seen. Only later did they realize how providential the timing was. A few weeks later the Turks attacked that section of Armenia; the two brides were the last people to leave their village alive.

Tiroon's welcome to Los Angeles must have been one of the strangest so young a wife ever experienced. Sirakan had not expected his father and the two women until the following day. He returned from the city dump to find a terrified-looking child standing in the living room. With a start he realized that this must be his wife — and that he himself was covered with dirt and grime from head to toe.

"Stay there!" he shouted at her. "Stay right there!" — as though the poor girl had anywhere else to go. He bolted for the rear of the house and half an hour later, scrubbed, brushed, and scented within an inch of his life, Sirakan "Sweetheart" Gabrielian made his formal speech of greeting to a very relieved young lady.

These were Rose's parents, the ones who would someday soon be choosing a husband for her. But I could never approach them directly with a request to marry their daughter. In my case as in hers, it was the family which must act.

How I trembled the night I broached the subject with mine. It was a June evening in 1932, and we were all seated around the dining-room table, the porch doors open to the breeze. "Dad, you know I'm nineteen now," I began.

Dad wiped his moustache and cut another piece of beef.

"And," I pressed on, "I'm about to graduate from high school. And I'm helping to make the farms pay. And you were nineteen when you got married."

My five sisters all stopped eating. Mother laid down her fork. There was a particular girl? she asked. Yes. Was she an Armenian? Yes. Then she was a Christian? Oh, yes.

"It's . . ." I began. "She's . . . it's Rose Gabrielian."

"Ahhh . . ." said Mother.

"So . . ." said Dad.

"Ohhh. . ." said all my sisters at once.

And so began the elaborate centuries-old process of making a proposal of marriage. First, although the families saw one another every week at church and were close friends, an official "meeting" must be arranged.

This delicate matter was always handled by a carefully selected go-between. After much discussion between them (I was not consulted of course), Mother and Dad agreed that the proper person for this sensitive task was Raphael Janoian the husband of Dad's sister Siroon. A good omen, I told myself, for of the six men who had married Dad's six sisters, Uncle Janoian was my favourite. He owned a large junkyard where, when I was fourteen, he'd let me rummage for the old car parts with which I'd built my first automobile. And this junkyard put him in daily contact with the Gabrielians' refuse hauling company.

I remember how I ran to meet his car as it turned into our driveway after his formal call on Sirakan Gabrielian. But Uncle Janoian was not going to discharge his trust so lightly. He proceeded to our living room with great deliberateness, accepted a cup of strong, sweet tea, and stirred it lengthily.

"Well, Raphael," Dad prompted.

"Well, Isaac," Uncle Janoian returned, "a date has been agreed upon. The Gabrielians will be delighted to receive a visit from the Shakarians on the twentieth of next month."

A visit agreed to! Then, at least, they had not rejected my suit automatically, and that must mean that Rose – that at any rate she was willing to consider me. My head swam with the thought.

At last the twentieth of July arrived. I finished my chores in the barn in record time and started to make ready. I bathed and showered and bathed again. I brushed my teeth until the enamel was loose. I used Listerine and Lavoris both. I scrubbed my farm-dirty nails till the bristles came off the brush.

I heard Dad back the Packard out of the garage. One last dash up the tile stairs to get a scuff mark off my shoe and dab extra styptic on the place where I'd nicked myself on the third shave.

"Demos!" Dad roared from the driveway. "What are you trying to do – be prettier than Rose?"

Wedged between my sisters in the back seat, I thought the seventeen miles between Downey and East Los Angeles had never seemed so long. At last we pulled up at 4311 Union Pacific. Up the gravel walk we trooped, past Tiroon Gabrielian's neat rows of basil, parsley, and other kitchen herbs. The front door swung open, and there they all stood: Sirakan and Tiroon, Rose's older brother Edward, uncles and great-aunts and cousins without number. And behind them all, Rose, in a summer dress the colour of her name.

I didn't have long to gaze at her, for the gathering broke up at once, Armenian fashion, into mutually exclusive groups, the men on one side of the large living room, the women on the other. Occasionally I would look over to where Rose was sitting with my sisters and wonder what girls talked about. Rose was the same age as my sister Lucy; I wondered if I would ever talk to Rose as naturally and easily as Lucy was doing.

Nor did I take any part in the solemn conversation going on in two overstuffed chairs drawn close together, between my father and Sirakan Gabrielian. Whatever passed between them, both men seemed satisfied; at the door Mr. Gabrielian said to Dad, "I will relay your messages to Rose."

And two weeks later Uncle Janoian delivered the momentous answer:

Rose would marry me.

Now came the five traditional nights of celebration at the bride's home for an answer of *yes*. They were joyous evenings of singing, eating, speech-making, and mutual congratu-

47

lations, for among Armenians it is not two individuals but two families who marry each other.

One evening Rose gave us a concert at the piano, and my heart swelled with pride to watch her fingers flying so swiftly over the keys. I had once taken violin lessons, but had stopped by mutual agreement of my teacher, myself, and everyone within hearing range. Florence had inherited both the violin and the lessons, and she too played for the assembled families – eight years old, her supple right arm crooked lovingly around the gleaming wood.

Another night came the giving of the "token," the customary gift from the boy to the girl, symbolising the new relationship. In this case it was a wristwatch set with diamonds. The gift had been chosen, again by my parents, but to me fell the task of crossing the room to where the ladies sat and fastening the watch around Rose's wrist. In the sudden silence, with every eye in the room upon me, my fingers turned to wood. First I couldn't get the tiny clasp open, then I couldn't get it shut. I thought longingly of the tractor shed where I could take a piece of machinery apart and put it together without a second thought. At last Rose reached over with her right hand and deftly fastened it for me.

And of course there were decisions for our elders to make, such as where the wedding would be held, and when. The church on Gless Street, all agreed, was far too small for the hundreds who would be coming – and besides, Orthodox friends and family would die rather than set foot there. No, the wedding would be at the groom's home, old-country fashion, and the feast which would follow (and which was, of course, the central event of any Armenian milestone) would be held in the big double tennis court in the back yard.

As to the date, the Gabrielians were adamant on waiting at least a year. Times had changed, they explained, since my mother had married at fifteen, and Rose's mother at thirteen.

A woman needed maturity to raise a family these days. We must wait until Rose was sixteen.

And all the while, as our affairs were discussed and decisions about our future made, Rose and I had yet to speak our first words to each other. Traditionally, that moment would come only after the formal engagement party to which more distant relatives and friends would be invited, these family get-togethers being preliminaries only.

But by the fourth night of celebration I could stand it no longer. Throwing tradition to the winds, I sprang to my feet.

"Mrs. Gabrielian," I said across the expanse of heads, "may I speak to Rose?"

For a horrified moment Tiroon Gabrielian stared at me in silence. Then with a shake of her head that asked what the younger generation was coming to, she led Rose and me into another room, placed two straight-backed chairs side by side in the centre of the floor, and went out, leaving us alone.

For the first time in our lives. And suddenly all the fine speeches I had rehearsed deserted me. I had planned masterpieces of feeling and expression – in my very best Armenian, because Sirakan Gabrielian, alarmed by the new "Hollywood madness" of the city, would permit no English spoken under his roof. I intended to tell her that she was the most beautiful girl in the world, and that I would spend my life trying to make her happy. But I couldn't remember a word, and I sat there tongue-tied and stupid. At last – to my horror – the words I blurted out were,

"Rose, I know God wants us together."

To my astonishment, her glowing brown eyes filled with tears. "Demos," she whispered, "all my life I've prayed that the man I married would say those words to me first of all."

Three weeks later came the official engagement party when the bride received the ring. We went together to a wholesale diamond house to pick it out, accompanied, of course, by a large contingent of family. The saleslady's name, I still remember, was Mrs. Earhart; we talked about her daughter, Amelia, who had just flown alone across the Atlantic Ocean. I caught Rose looking wistfully at a lovely small diamond on one of the trays, but my mother chose a different one. It never occurred to either of us to question her decision.

The engagement party was a sit-down dinner for three hundred, held in a grocery store owned by the Gabrielians. After this it was permissible for me to call on Rose as often as I liked, which was every nignt I wasn't working, usually bearing Mother's buttery, diamond-shaped *paklava* or *shakar lokoom*.

As the long year passed, Mother, Rose and my sisters went shopping oftener and oftener. By tradition the groom's family buys the wardrobe for the bride, and selecting a hand-bag or a hat could take half a dozen excursions. Rose's favourite purchase was a dark maroon dress with matching shoes. In the Armenian community only married women wore dark colours; Rose was convinced she would look five years older the minute she put them on.

The wedding took place August 6, 1933. That morning the entire Shakarian clan drove into East Los Angeles to "bring the bride home." Since the main meal of the day was to be in the evening, the Gabrielians served only a five-course luncheon, a mere snack by Armenian standards. Then both families set out for Downey in a flower-decked caravan of twenty-five cars.

At home the fence around the tennis court had vanished beneath cascades of roses. Of the rest of the day I recall only isolated moments. Pastor Perumean's long light-brown beard bobbing up and down as he read the ancient Armenian ser-vice. Strings of electric light bulbs looped between the palm trees, and white-jacketed waiters struggling under the tremendous platters of *shishkebab* and the traditional date-and-almond wedding *pilaf* which Mother had been preparing for days.

I do remember that there were five hundred guests, and every one of them it seemed, had written a poem in Armenian which must be heard and applauded by the entire gathering. By eleven P.M. I was dizzy with fatigue, and there were tears in Rose's eyes because she'd had on her tight white shoes since morning.

But as we stood in the endless receiving line saying goodnight to friends and family, we were sure of one thing. Rose and I were finally, thoroughly, irrevocably, permanently married – in the most Armenian sense of the word.

3

Time Bomb

It was the tradition – which is to say we did it without question – for the bride and groom to spend the first year or two of their married lives with the groom's family. The shadow over the big Spanish house during this time was my sister Lucy's health. At eleven, she had suffered a chest injury in a school bus accident; increasingly now she complained of difficulty breathing. Nothing that surgery could do, nothing that prayer could do, seemed to bring permanent healing. "Why, God?" I asked over and over. "Why did You heal Florence's elbow, but don't heal Lucy's chest?"

Rose and I were living with my family when our son, Richard, was born in October, 1934. At once we started building a home of our own next door. The next few years were challenging ones at the dairies. Even during the depression the business was growing bigger than Dad had ever dreamed, as he laboured in the leather dust of the harness factory, or urged Jack along with a wagonload of vegetables. Already we were the largest dairy in California, and Dad had a new dream – to be the biggest in the world. We were told that nowhere in the world was there a dairy milking three thousand cows. This became our goal.

Along with this dream went others. We would expand our

milk haulage fleet. Already we had three hundred trucks. With five hundred we could serve the entire state. We could also use our fleet to haul silage. And to get our hogs and beef cattle to the meat processing plants. The heady ambitions spun higher and higher. Why, in America there was no limit to what a practical hard-working Armenian could achieve.

And probably would achieve, furthermore. I took as my special project the building of "Reliance Number Three" — the third of our dairies, which was to bring our capacity to three thousand head. We bought a forty-acre tract and I began the construction of corrals, silos, and a modern barn and creamery where milk flowed from cow to bottle without ever being touched by hand.

Every now and then I wondered — briefly — if God still had that plan for my life I'd felt so sure of when I was a boy. But the fact was, God was no longer squarely at the centre of my life. Of course we still drove into Gless Street each Sunday, little Richard bouncing on the back seat. But when I was honest with myself I knew that the business was the real focus of my thoughts and energies. It was not at all unusual for me to start work at seven in the morning and finish at eleven at night.

In 1936 I launched a new enterprise — a fertilizer plant — and from then on I often sat at my desk right through the night.

Even when I prayed, the prayers were apt to concern the price of alfalfa, or the gas mileage our trucks were getting. For instance, there were those all-important decisions every dairyman faces: selecting the right breeding stock. A quality bull, even back in the mid thirties, could cost fifteen thousand. But in spite of such a price tag, backed by a blue-ribbon pedigree, buying a bull was a gamble. The unknown was whether the animal could transmit his desirable qualities to his offspring — a bull who can consistently do so is one in a thousand.

So I would pray, in the noise and dust of the auction ring, "Lord, You made these animals, You see every cell and fibre. Show me which bull to buy." Many a time I picked the scrawniest little bullcalf in the pen and saw him develop into a breeder of champions.

And I was forever bringing my Pentecostal beliefs into the cow barns. Many nights I laid my hand on a feverish calf, or a cow in difficult labour, and watched the vet stare in amazement as prayer did what he could not.

Yes, I still believed, all right. The *Reliance* in our company name meant reliance on God, and we did rely on Him, every day. It was just that I seemed to be on the taking end all the time, with very little giving out.

Which is why I was so puzzled by the prophecy which was spoken over Rose and me.

Milton Hansen was a house painter – at a time when nobody was getting his house painted. A tall, thin, fair-haired Norwegian, he'd had more than his share of griefs, and yet was the most joyful human being I'd ever known. We always knew when he was coming to visit because we could hear him far down the street, roaring a gospel hymn at the top of his lungs.

One night when Rose and Milton and I were sitting in our small living room, Milton suddenly raised his long arms and began to shake. Milton belonged to a particular tradition among Pentecostals: when the Spirit descended on him he would close his eyes, lift his hands, and speak in a loud, oratorical voice. Rose and I were "chosen vessels" he thundered now. We were "being guided step by step".

"Keep your mind on the things of God," Milton declaimed. "You will enter through the city gate and no one will shut it against you. You will speak of holy matters with heads of state around the world." I looked at Rose and saw that she was as astonished as I. Important statesmen?

World travel? Neither Rose nor I had ever been outside California. And with a three-year-old child and another baby on the way, our hopes and dreams were built squarely around our own small household.

Milton must have seen the look on our faces. "Don't blame me, folks," he said in his ordinary kindly tones. "I'm just repeating what the Lord said. I don't understand it either."

I'm sure I would have forgotten Milton's prophecy almost at once, if it hadn't been for a second surprising experience. Several days later, on impulse, I dropped into a midweek church service in a part of the city where I had never been before. At the close of the sermon was an altar call. Perhaps because I knew my spiritual life was not what it should be, I went forward and knelt at the rail. The pastor came down the line of kneeling people laying hands on one after the other. When he came to me he said in a voice that carried all over the church:

"My son, you are a vessel chosen for a specific work. I am guiding you. You will visit high government officials in many parts of the world in the name of the Lord. When you arrive at a city the gates will open and no man will be able to close them."

I got to my feet a little unsteadily. What an incredible coincidence! This minister could not conceivably know me or Milton Hansen. Could God Himself really be giving me a message? And such an incomprehensible one. "Keep your mind on the things of God," Milton had said. I knew that was sound theology. And I also knew that my mind, try as I might, was more apt to be fixed on the affairs of the Shakarian family.

The following year brought two milestones to that family. The first was the birth of our daughter, Geraldine, in October, 1938. And the second, the following spring, the death of my sister Lucy at age twenty-two. She was just Rose's age, the most beautiful of all my sisters, a sensitive and brilliant girl whose dream – unusual among Armenian girls in those days – had been to be a schoolteacher. Whittier College, which she had attended, closed down the day of her funeral, an unheard-of tribute. And for the first time in several years I found myself asking again the big questions. What are we here for? What is the meaning of death? Of life?

I looked around the Gless Street church at friends and family gathered for the customary funeral meal, and wondered about these things. Death, among Armenians, was the signal for all the relatives to assemble, from the immediate family to the most distant cousin-by-marriage twice-removed. After the burial, tradition decreed a formal sit-down dinner. In Armenia where relatives might have one hundred miles to return home over rugged mountain tracks, the meal had been a necessity. Here in California, the funeral dinner became a sacrament of family unity.

I sat beside Dad at one end of the long table which had been set up in the sanctuary and looked down to where Mother sat at the other. Next to her was Rose, Baby Gerry on her lap, four-year-old Richard beside her. Uncle Magardich Mushegan had died some years before, but next to Richard sat Magardich's son Aram, and then Aram's son Harry. And there were Dad's six sisters and their husbands, and my own four remaining sisters, Ruth, Grace, and Roxanne with husbands and families of their own. Even Florence, I saw with a start, was – by Armenian standards – a grown woman of 15. And at other tables around the room, nieces, and cousins and in-laws without end.

And everyone of us had prospered. These were strong people, proud people, the men with stout well-fed stomachs, the women in rustling black silk. I thought about the prophecy that had brought each person in this room to this abundant land. "I will bless you and prosper you," God had promised, back in Kara Kala, and looking around me I could see that He had.

But there had been another part to the prophecy: "I will cause your seed to be a blessing to the nations." Were we fulfilling that part too? Were we blessing anyone? In a way, of course. These people were all good neighbours, good workers, good employers. But . . . was that all?

"It can't be all," I said to Rose as we drove home to Downey. "I know God is asking us to do something for other people. Only I don't know what."

And so over the next few months I began really paying attention to the men I worked with every day. There were a lot of them – not just our own cowhands, but grain salesmen, truck drivers, bottle suppliers. And I made an amazing discovery.

These men never spoke about God.

It was a while before my mind could take it in. God was as real to me as . . . as Rose and the children. He was part of every moment of every day. Of course I'd known, in an abstract way, that there were people who didn't know Him. That's what the missionary collection went for – islands in the Pacific someplace.

But that right here in Los Angeles – where there were churches on every corner – there could be grown men who didn't believe, was something that had never even occurred to me. And now that it had, what was I to do?

It was while I was praying about this one night that a truly terrifying scene popped into my mind. The setting was Lincoln Park, a big open area with lots of grass and trees ten miles from Downey, where we often went for picnics. On a Sunday afternoon in summertime there might be four thousand people sitting around on blankets. But in the picture that suddenly appeared in my mind's eye, I had somehow climbed up on a platform in the middle of all these people and was talking to them about Jesus.

The next morning, instead of vanishing with a good night's sleep the ridiculous idea was still there. As I put on my tie I mentioned it to Rose.

"Honey, I keep imagining this wild scene where I'm standing up on a platform talking to a crowd of people. . . ."

". . . in Lincoln Park!" she finished for me.

I turned from the mirror, thumb still hooked through the tie.

"I've been thinking the very same thing!" she said. "I haven't been able to get it out of my mind. It seemed so crazy I didn't want to tell you."

We stood blinking at each other in the sunny bedroom, little thinking how often we were to experience this phenomenon. At the time it seemed only an outlandish coincidence – and a pointless one at that.

"You know me, Rose. If I have to speak to more than two people at once I get so tongue-tied I can't remember my own name." I was a dairy farmer, slow thinking, slower talking. I knew I could never put into words what Jesus meant to me.

It was Rose who would not let the idea go. "Remember, we've been asking God what we're to do. What if this is His answer? Otherwise how could both of us have had such a strange idea at the same time?"

Well, I checked into city regulations and found to my relief that Lincoln Park was reserved for public recreation: no private use whatever could be made of it.

But Rose, looking about on her own, discovered an empty lot across the street in full view of the park. It belonged to a man who owned an ostrich farm set up hopefully to attract customers from the park. Business wasn't too brisk, and he would be delighted to rent out the vacant lot beside the farm on Sunday afternoons.

And so – suddenly – hardly knowing how it had happened – I found myself committed to actually doing this crazy thing. At first there were so many practical details to attend to that I didn't have time to be scared. There were police permits to obtain, a speaker's stand to erect, amplifying equipment to rent. Rose thought she could get several girls from church to come and sing.

As for the talks, I comforted myself that I had heard so many sermons in my life that surely a little fluency had rubbed off, and the music could fill most of the time.

But as the first Sunday drew close, I started waking up at night, sweating. The dream was always the same: I was standing on a ridiculously tall platform, shouting and waving my arms about, while looking on in horror stood some fellow I had done business with that day.

Suppose it really happened? Suppose some buyer or salesman really should be in the park? What would he think? Here I was – a successful young businessman – beginning to be asked into the right civic organizations, beginning to get a reputation for good judgment. What if the word got around that I was some kind of religious fanatic? It could ruin not only my name but everything Dad had worked so long to build up.

And then it was the first Sunday in June, 1940, the day we'd arranged to start. We drove out to the lot beside the ostrich farm after the morning service at church, and set up the public address system. It was a warm, cloudless day and across the street Lincoln Park was jammed. Why couldn't it have rained? I kept thinking as Rose raved about the beautiful weather. Now she was leading three girls from church in the familiar hymn "What a Friend We Have in Jesus." The song ended. I climbed the three homemade steps to the platform, clutched the microphone and cleared my throat. To my horror the sound boomed out over the loudspeakers. I stepped back a pace.

"Friends ..." I began. Again a roar of sound exploded around me. I stumbled through a few sentences, conscious only of the monstrous, mechanical echo of my own voice, then signalled desperately for the girls to sing again.

Here and there people were picking up their blankets and I was sure we were driving them out of the park. But to my surprise most of them were moving closer, settling down where they could see us better. With an actual audience in sight my courage rose. I stepped back to the microphone, selected one poor fellow in a yellow polo shirt, riveted my eyes on his, and directed my sermon straight at him.

And then I heard it. A woman's voice, clear and carrying: "Darling, isn't that Demos Shakarian?"

My eyes searched the crowd. There she was, pointing at me across a picnic hamper while beside her, squinting near-sightedly, sat the man from whom we bought electrified fencing.

"It can't be Shakarian," he said in the sudden silence. He was fumbling in his shirt pocket. He pulled out a pair of glasses.

"By jimminy, it *is* Shakarian!"

My collar was cutting into my windpipe. The microphone was wet and slippery in my hands. I heard a sob and wondered if I was crying. I looked down. There beside the little platform stood the man in the yellow shirt, tears streaming down his cheeks.

"Oh, you're right, brother, you're right!" he sobbed. "God has been good to me!"

I stared down at him, dumbfounded. Luckily Rose had the presence of mind to invite him up onto the platform. He took the sweaty microphone from my hands and poured out a long story of material success and personal failure. A little stream of people was crossing the street to cluster around the platform.

"That's my story, too!" said another man, and he too, climbed the three stairs. I forgot about the loudspeakers, I forgot about the man who sold fences. I thought only of the wonder that God was at work in Lincoln Park. When we packed away the equipment at the end of the afternoon, six people had given their lives to Him.

For three months, all through June, July, and August, 1940, we followed the same routine each Sunday, arriving across from the park around two P.M., staying till five or six. Soon a pattern developed. There were generally a few hecklers, a few supporters who shushed the hecklers, and one old man who was regularly delivered from drink. The number of people who came to the platform was never very large. Four. Ten. A dozen. And while we occasionally kept in touch with them, most of the time there was no way of knowing if real changes in their lives followed or not.

But if the outward effects of these Sunday afternoons were hard to measure, the inward ones, on me, were very clear. I had gone into the meetings worried about my own dignity; I came out of them knowing I had none. God's answer to my fear that someone I knew would see me, had been to bring to the park one by one, Sunday after Sunday, just about every man I'd ever done business with.

There, He seemed to be saying. *You've made a fool of yourself in front of* him. *There's one less person you have to bother impressing.*

Later, when I'd run into the man at a Lions Club meeting or a Kiwanis affair, there was generally an awkward silence, occasionally a burst of laughter – and not much more. None of the business disasters I had vaguely imagined ever materialised. By the end of the summer I had learned a lesson

I would never forget: "What people will think" is largely a bogeyman of our own self-centredness.

There was another kind of resistance that summer, however, and it came from the direction Rose and I least expected it: the church on Gless Street. At first the Elders seemed to regard these Sunday afternoon "outings" as a kind of summer madness on the part of the young. But as the meetings continued week after week, the older people began to protest.

One elderly man spoke for them all one Sunday morning in August, rising from the front bench to warn us against continuing in Lincoln Park.

"It's not right!" he proclaimed, his long grey beard jerking with emotion. "It's . . . it's un-Armenian!"

And suddenly I knew that he was right. I pictured Armenia down through the ages, that small embattled country clinging to the lonely truth through conquest and massacre, surrounded always by bigger, stronger, unbelieving nations, finding its strength through turning inward.

If Rose and I, now, were being told to turn outward, we would have to do it largely on our own. For the first time in our lives we found ourselves in conflict with our parents' generation. The world, as we looked out over the blankets of Lincoln Park that summer, was a far bigger place than we had supposed. And a far, far lonelier one.

In September the days grew cooler, the crowds in the park dropped off, we stopped holding meetings. The dairy, anyhow, was occupying more and more time as I got ready to launch a new kind of milk merchandising. Why not, I asked myself, start a drive-in milk service on the highway at Reliance Number Three? We could sell our product for pennies less a quart than it could be delivered to the home, or purchased at a store.

To let the public know about our idea we held a Grand Opening with accompanying fanfare. Advertisements in the papers, announcements over the radio, flyers in the mail. At the dairy itself, banners, music, well-known entertainers. Business started with a bang and remained that way. Immediately I began to dream of a chain of such outlets across California. It would make us wealthy.

But the headiest prospect of all for the Shakarian fortunes came in connection with our new milling operation.

Little did I realise that the situation was also a time bomb.

Getting into the milling business had seemed like such a natural outgrowth of the dairies. A milk cow will eat twenty pounds of grain a day, plus thirty pounds of hay. Multiply this by the three thousand cows which we were hoping someday soon to have, and you get the incredible figure of 150 thousand pounds of hay and grain ration every day!

For years we'd been buying feed from local milling operators, then mixing the grain ourselves according to a formula we'd developed which produced an unusually rich milk.

The results were so good in fact that nearby dairymen had begun to ask Dad:

"Isaac, do you think you could sell us some of your special mix?"

"I don't know why not," Dad said.

It seemed like a logical next step for the business. We would be able to buy grain in much larger quantities, thus reducing the cost to our own dairies. With the increased volume, we could do our own milling, cutting costs still further. And we'd make a small but steady profit on the grain we sold other dairies.

And so, we began the new expansion with great expectations. We purchased a milling operation near one of our farms, consisting of three sixty-foot grain elevators which had been used for corn silage. We emptied them, washed them down, reinforced them with new layers of cement.

I foresaw a wonderful future for the new venture. The Southern Pacific Railroad tracks went right past these elevators. Always in the past, grain had been transferred from boxcar to elevator by a complicated system of trucks, augurs, and hand-shovelling. During our first year in milling I perfected a system for moving the grain directly to the elevators by the use of huge vacuums. Under the old methods it had taken three men an entire day to empty a forty-ton boxcar; with the new system a single man could do the same job in two and a half hours. We cut our handling costs by 80 percent and created quite a stir in the industry.

I loved to go out to the mill. The hum of the machinery, the whir of the vacuum, the freights rattling by, even the fine dust which settled over the gleaming black finish of my new Cadillac – all of this was intoxication to me.

And yet, as I say, built into the whole operation was a tremendous trap.

It had to do with the nature of commodities. Commodities fluctuate madly in price. People who speculate in oats and wheat and barley can make – and lose – immense fortunes within a few hours. On Wall Street there are experts who specialize in just such speculations. But a farmer, who deals with the actual physical grain itself, is also a speculator whether he likes it or not.

It works this way: I buy grain on say, the first of July for delivery the following fall. I pay the current July price, knowing that by fall the price of the commodity will probably have changed. If I've bought the grain in July at $2.00 per hundred pounds, and by fall the price has dropped to $1.50, I have lost. If, however, the price has risen to $2.50, then I have gained. Part of being a good milling operator is to buy heavily when you expect the price to go up, hold back when you expect a drop.

I knew this in theory, that winter of 1940-41. I had yet to learn what it was like in experience.

4

The Man Who
Changed His Mind

As the warmer weather brought people out into the parks
the next spring, Rose and I began talking about meetings.
"But not just Sunday afternoons," she said. "people get
interested and then we pack up and go home and nothing
happens for a week."

What if we held meetings in the evenings? Every evening.
If we could set up a tent somewhere we could have meetings
rain or shine.

"On the church property!" we both said at once – and
laughed because that coincidence had happened again. For
quite a while now the building on Gless Street had been too
small for the growing Armenian community, and the church
had recently purchased an empty lot on the corner of Goodrich Boulevard and Carolina Place in East Los Angeles
where they planned to build.

And so we set about trying to get the Elders' permission.
All the suspicion and bafflement of the previous summer
sprang again into those lined brown faces. Who were these
strangers we were so interested in? Why should the
Armenian Pentecostal Church get involved?

It wouldn't be our church only, we explained. Our idea
was that all the Pentecostal churches in the area should

sponsor the meetings. Our church could provide the tent site, another one could provide musicians or ushers. We'd work together.

But at the word *together* the faces grew more guarded still. *Together?* With the Foursquare Church, and the Assemblies of God, and the Pentecostal Holiness people, with their dubious doctrines? Why, some of these so-called Christian groups actually had men and women sitting side by side! And the old men would be off, talking about what seemed to us secondary matters, while Rose and I sat silent, our summer project forgotten.

For the fact was that the wind of Pentecost, which had blown out of Russia into Armenia nearly a century before, had dwindled by now into a denomination as rigid as any other. It was always this way. All through history, each fresh outpouring of the Spirit soon became, in human hands, a new orthodoxy. The great revival on Azusa Street for example, here in this very city, which started out in freedom and joy and a breaking down of barriers, had solidified by the 1940s into a number of self-contained churches who couldn't communicate even with each other – let alone the world as a whole.

The tragedy, as Rose and I saw it, was that they had so much to give. Each little group, behind its own walls, was experiencing each week the power of God to provide, to heal, to guide, while the world which so desperately needed this power – the men I dealt with six days a week – didn't know it existed.

"Then you don't need to get involved at all," I begged the Elders. "I'll arrange about the tent and the clean-up and everything. Just let us use the land."

In the end it wasn't anything I said that moved them, but the fact that Dad spoke for the project. The name Isaac Shakarian carried weight in the church. If Isaac was for it – well, risky as it sounded, it must be all right.

So, we got our permission. And at once almost regretted it. Setting up a tent, we learned, was going to be a far different matter from knocking together a speaker's stand. Renting the tent itself was the easiest part. It was to be "a place of public accommodation," and there were as many regulations to comply with as for a permanent building. I had to appear before the Zoning Board, the Fire Department, the Police Department, the Sanitation Board, the Light and Power Commission – and each time explain all over again what I was proposing and why.

Only when I had this fistful of permits could the actual fitting out of the tent begin. Now all electric wiring had to be inspected, aisles and exits conformed to specific standards, trash receptacles and portable toilets provided, water trucks hired to keep down the dust. Then there was the job of letting people know. Radio spots, newspaper ads, posters in store windows – I tried to remember everything I'd learned when we opened our drive-in milk outlet.

All of this took money, all of this took time. At last even Dad grew impatient. I'd scarcely been in the office for weeks, he reminded me. He didn't need to say what was uppermost in both our minds: the fertilizer plant, which had been my first independent project, was losing money. For five years I'd struggled to make it a paying proposition; if it was to survive, I'd have to throw all my time and energy into it right now. And yet I could not shake the feeling that these tent meetings were important too.

The evening services began in July and ran every night for six weeks. I had learned for sure the summer before that I was no speaker. My heart was full of the wonder and reality of God, but my mouth could never find the words. Harry Mushegan, my young second cousin, was different. Like his father Aram and his grandfather Kagardich, he had the commanding manner, the ringing phrase, that made people sit up and take notice. He was only twenty but already he was a better speaker than I would ever be, and we asked him to do the preaching.

People came, and they came back, and as the weeks went on the crowds grew. The five Pentecostal denominations who had so gingerly joined together to sponsor the evenings began gradually to catch the spark. Their pastors sat on the platform, with Rose at the piano, their choirs led the singing.

Nights when no choir came, Florence sang for us in her high, sweet, professionally trained soprano. Florence had graduated from high school in June, and was looking forward to entering Whittier College in the fall. As for me, I helped out where I could. I conducted the meetings, made phone calls, arranged transportation, kept the books.

A little to everyone's surprise, those books now showed entries under *Income* as well as *Outgo*. Late each evening when the pastors' committee counted the offering money, it totalled more than the night before. It was amazing, as we never made a big pitch for donations. It was also ironic. Every time I checked with the bookkeeper at the fertilizer plant, those accounts were doing worse.

Out of the offerings we paid for newspaper and radio ads and the rental on the tent, and still there was money left over. For most of the expenses I'd kept no records, never expecting to get them back. Now I had an idea. What if the rest of the collections were to go into a special bank account administered jointly by the five churches?

In mid-August the tent came down, volunteers cleaned up the site. Hundreds of people had heard for the first time the message that God is real. Some had made the decision to become Christians. A fertilizer business in Downey had closed its doors for the last time.

But the furthest-reaching effect, as it happened, grew out of that little bank account. In order to make decisions about it, the pastor of the Foursquare Church telephoned the pastor of the Pentecostal Church of God. An Elder of the Assemblies of God was seen having lunch with an Elder of the Armenian Pentecostal Church. And both of them actually walked through the door and sat down to worship with the Pentecostal Holiness congregation down the street. . . .

It was a Tuesday morning in late September and I was sitting at my desk, trying to pull some kind of order out of the shambles of my business affairs. At first I scarcely heard the telephone ringing at my elbow; when I picked it up it was several seconds before I realized that the person at the other end was crying. It was Rose.

". . . Downey Hospital," she was saying, "as quick as you can."

"What? Who?" I said stupidly.

"Florence!" she repeated. "Driving to Whittier this morning. You remember how foggy it was – oh, Demos she must never have seen the truck at all."

Still not taking it in, I ran for my car and covered the few blocks to Downey Hospital in a daze. Most of the family had already reached the little one-storey wooden building. Florence was on the operating table, Dad told me, but there wasn't much the doctors could do. Dad was having trouble talking, and it was my sister Ruth's husband who filled in the details for me.

The accident had happened at 7:30 A.M. in one of the thick grey fogs that creep in from the Pacific on fall mornings. Apparently Florence had failed to see a stop sign, her car had collided with a road repair truck, spilling tons of boiling asphalt across the highway. The driver of the truck was unhurt but Florence had been thrown from her car onto the flaming tar. A passerby had pulled her off and rolled her in his coat jacket, but not before her entire back had been critically burned.

It was these massive burns that prevented the surgeon now from setting the broken bones. At last she was transferred to Intensive Care and we were permitted, one by one, to stand in the doorway and look in. It was Dr. Haygood who led us down the corridor, weeping as unashamedly as any of us. It was this skilled man who had brought Florence into the world seventeen years before, and doctored her through the measles and whooping cough of childhood. Now all he could do was pat Mother's hand over and over:

"She's strong and young, Zahouri," he kept saying. "She has a tremendous will to live."

When it came my turn to step to the doorway I could scarcely believe it was Florence on the high hospital bed: Florence with the pixie face and angel's voice, youngest and most gifted of the family, suspended by pulleys and weights in a bed of salve. Her eyes were closed and a continual moan came from her throat.

"Lord God!" I prayed. "Don't let her hurt! Take the pain away!"

Was I imagining it, or had the groaning stopped for a moment? "Take away the pain," I prayed again.

Rose and I returned home to give Richard and Gerry their lunch. When I returned to the hospital that afternoon Florence was crying out with the pain, though still apparently unconscious to everything else. Again I stood in the doorway and prayed, again the cries subsided. The rest of that day and evening, whenever the pain was worst, my prayers seemed to help. Even the doctors and nurses noticed it.

"Demos," Dr. Haygood told me, "you can come into this room whenever you like. Even the intravenous feeding seems to go better when you're here."

So I was fitted out with a white gown, mask, and surgical

71

cap, and a chair for me placed beside the bed. For the next five days I spent every possible moment in that room. As consciousness returned, the pain grew more excruciating. No drug, no amount of shots seemed to help; the only time Florence slept, the nurses reported, was during my visits.

Why this should be so I had no idea. Often, as I sat there, my mind went back eleven years to the time when she had broken her elbow and I had known, one morning in church, that she would be healed. Some strange link seemed to exist between Florence and me – and yet this time healing did not follow my prayers. Temporary relief from pain, but not an end to the danger she was in.

Because now the real peril appeared. X rays taken immediately after the accident showed that her left hip and pelvis had been crushed by the impact with the pavement. Since then new X rays showed fragments of the splintered bone travelling toward the vital organs of the abdomen. Every day a fresh photograph was taken; every day looking at the slides with the doctors, I saw the needle-sharp splinters working deeper into the abdominal cavity.

Six days after the accident, when the burns still would not permit an operation, our church declared a day-long fast. Starting at midnight Sunday, the entire congregation touched neither food nor water. At 7:00 Monday evening, still fasting, they gathered at the just-finished church on Goodrich Boulevard in East Los Angeles to complete the twenty-four-hour vigil for Florence's healing "with one accord in one place," as the Book of Acts puts it (2:1).

I alone was not with them. I had a special mission that night in the town of Maywood, five miles from Downey. For months now we had been hearing about a man named Charles Price. Some years back, Dr. Price had been the pastor of a large Congregational church up in Lodi, California – an ultramodern minister with an ultramodern church plant even boasting a bowling alley. Then the evangelist Aimee Semple McPherson visited the area. Dr. Price went to her tent meeting armed with pad and pencil to take notes of all the silly Pentecostal claims Miss McPherson would be spouting, so that he could warn his congregation against her. Halfway through the service the pad and pencil were back in his pocket, and Dr. Price was on his knees, tears streaming down his cheeks, hands raised above his head, praising God in an unknown tongue.

From that night on Charles Price's ministry was radically changed. He called his new message "the full gospel," by which he meant that no part of the New Testament message would henceforth be left out of his preaching. He became known especially for his insistence that healings like the ones recorded in the Bible were meant to be part of the normal experience of the church in every age.

And now Dr. Price was in nearby Maywood holding a tent meeting of his own. As I neared the spot, my heart sank. Cars were parked half a mile away, and when I finally reached the huge tent, every seat was taken with scores standing on the grass outside.

Dr. Price was speaking from a platform hung with red and white bunting, a sandy-haired middle-aged man with rimless spectacles that glittered in the overhead spotlights. He finished his sermon and invited any in need of healing to come forward for prayers. Hundreds of people surged into the aisles. I looked at my watch. It was nine P.M. I would never get near him tonight. But the thought of my church on their knees before God made me stay. Slowly the long lines inched forward. Ten. Ten-thirty. Eleven. The ushers were trying to close the meeting. "Dr. Price will be glad to pray with you tomorrow night, brother."

Dr. Price was gathering up his Bible and the bottle of oil with which he anointed the sick. "Sir!" I called out.

He turned and squinted to see past the bright lights.

I dodged past an usher. "Dr. Price, my name is Demos Shakarian, and my sister's been in an automobile accident, and the doctors in Downey Hospital say she can't live, and we wondered if you'd come," I said, getting it all out in one breath.

Dr. Price closed his eyes and I saw the weariness in his face. He remained standing there a moment. Then abruptly opened his eyes.

"I will come," he said.

I hurried ahead of him through the slowly dispersing crowd, fretting each time someone stopped him. Dr. Price noticed my impatience.

"Don't be anxious, son," he said. "Your sister will be healed tonight."

I stared at the man. How could he make such a blandly certain statement? But of course, I reminded myself, he hadn't seen the X rays; he couldn't have any idea how serious the situation was.

My scepticism must have showed in my face, because as I started up the motor he said, "Let me tell you, young man, why I am so sure your sister will be healed." Years before, he related, back in 1924, a short while after his experience in Miss McPherson's meeting, he had been motoring through Canada when he came to the little town of Paris, Ontario. As he drove through the village he felt a strange urging to turn to the right. He did so. Then he felt a compelling urge to turn left. In this manner Dr. Price was guided through the town until he came abreast of the Methodist church. There he seemed to get the order: *Stop.*

Without any idea why he was doing so, Charles Price rang the doorbell of the pastor's house next door and introduced himself. He was, he said, an evangelist – and suddenly he heard himself asking if he could hold a series of meetings in this church. Much to Dr. Price's surprise, the pastor said *yes*.

Among the people who attended the meetings, Dr. Price's attention was especially drawn to a pathetically crippled young woman, whose husband carried her in each evening, and laid her on a cushion on one of the front benches. Inquiring about them, he learned that their names were Louis and Eva Johnston, that they came from Laurel, Ontario, and that Eva Johnston had been bedridden and in constant pain for over ten years following an attack of rheumatic fever. Dr. Price kept looking down at those shrivelled and twisted legs, the right one grotesquely drawn behind the other. The couple had gone to twenty different doctors in Toronto, he was told; they'd tried electric treatments, X rays, surgery, heat massage, only to have the deformity grow worse each year. And yet – as he preached – Dr. Price knew that tonight Eva Johnston was going to be healed. He knew because each time he looked toward her he felt physical warmth envelop him, like a heavy blanket settling over his shoulders.

A shiver ran down my spine as I recalled my identical experience with Florence's elbow. With difficulty I kept my eyes on the road ahead.

Dr. Price interpreted the sensation of weight and warmth as the Presence of God. He told the congregation that they were about to witness a very special miracle. He stepped down from the platform, laid his hands on the woman's head, and began to pray. Before the entire congregation, the woman's back drew erect, the twisted legs straightened and grew visibly longer, and although she had not taken a step for over ten years, Eva Wilson Johnston got to her feet and walked – almost danced – the entire length of the aisle. Dr. Price was still in touch with the Johnstons; the healing had been permanent.

"And tonight," Charles Price went on, "we are going to

see another miracle, because the moment you spoke to me that 'blanket' fell over my shoulders again. It's there now. God is in this situation."

I swallowed hard, for a moment not trusting myself to speak. In the eleven years since my own experience I had never heard of a similar thing.

It was half past eleven when we reached Downey. The front door to the little thirty-three-bed hospital was locked and we had to ring the bell. At last a nurse appeared. "I'm glad you're here," she told me. "Florence is bad tonight."

I asked if Dr. Price might come with me into the room and he, too, was fitted out with a sterile gown and mask. Then the two of us entered Florence's room.

She lay in her bed of salve, half hidden by a thicket of tubes and pulley wires. I introduced Charles to her and she nodded weakly.

Doctor Price took the bottle of oil from his pocket and poured a little in his hand. Then reaching through the apparatus around the bed, he placed his fingertips on Florence's forehead. "Lord Jesus," he said, "we thank You for being here. We thank You for healing our sister."

His strong gentle voice continued to pray but I no longer heard the words. For an extraordinary change had come over the atmosphere in the room. It seemed more ... more *crowded* somehow. The air itself seemed to have become thick, almost as though we were standing in water.

All at once, on the high bed, Florence twisted. Dr. Price jumped back as one of the heavy steel traction weights swung past his head. Florence rolled to one side as far as the wires would allow, then to the other. Now weights all over the room were swinging, circling, as she rocked back and forth. I knew I should try to stop her – doctors had said over and over that the shattered hip must remain immobile. But I stayed where I was, wrapped and bathed in that pulsing air.

A groan came from deep in Florence's throat, but whether of pain or a kind of wordless ecstasy, I could not tell. For twenty incredible minutes Florence continued to toss and roll in her wire prison, while Dr. Price and I dodged the wildly swinging weights. At every second I expected a nurse to burst through the doorway and demand to know what we were doing; I knew the room was checked every ten minutes. But no one came; it was as though the three of us had been transported out of ordinary space and time altogether into a world inhabited only by that warm all-invading Presence.

And just as suddenly, it was an ordinary hospital room again. Florence lay still on the bed, gradually the weights ceased their circling. For a long moment she stared at me.

"Demos," she whispered, "Jesus healed me."

I bent down above her. "I know," I said.

When the nurse stepped into the room a few minutes later, she was delighted to find Florence sleeping soundly....

The next morning, after driving Dr. Price to his home in Pasadena, I was still asleep when Dr. Haygood phoned.

"I want you to come down and look at these X rays," was all he would say.

The X-ray room was jammed when I arrived, doctors, nurses, lab technicians all crowding to see. Pinned against a lighted screen were eight X-ray plates. The first seven showed a crushed and dislocated left hip and pelvis. The bone was almost pulverized in places, the bone chips more widely dispersed in each succeeding photograph. The eighth slide, taken that morning, showed a pelvis that was normal in every respect. The two sides of the picture were identical: the left hip bone as well formed as the right. Only some hair-fine lines indicated that once – surely many years ago – this solid bone had ever been injured.

Florence remained in the hospital another month while the burns on her back continued to heal. The night before she was discharged she had a dream, a strange one in which twenty-five glasses of water stood on a table for her to drink. "I believe those are the years I'm to have here on earth," she told Rose and me when we came next day to bring her home. "I believe God is giving me twenty-five more years in which to serve Him."

I didn't know about that. I only knew that with my own eyes I had seen God's power.

What I had yet to learn was my own weakness.

5

Handhold in Heaven

December, 1941. The United States was at war. With the attack on Pearl Harbour, Los Angeles overnight became the centre of round-the-clock defence activity. By day the freeways were jammed with olive-green army trucks; by night the city hurried about its work in the eerie darkness of a total blackout, and we did the pre-dawn milking in barns with shades nailed to the windows. The small Northamerican Aircraft factory near us in Downey mushroomed into a huge barbed-wire enclosed plant, cars and trucks pouring through the gates twenty-four hours a day. To Rose's despair and seven-year-old Richard's delight, the anti-aircraft installations went up almost in our front yard.

Because dairies were classed as essential industry, dairymen were not drafted. But before long many of our employees and suppliers were in the services or the defence plants. I divided my time between the calf pens and cow barns, wherever we were shortest handed, and the various ration boards and allocations offices, begging the fuel, grain, tyres, and truck parts we needed to keep going.

The toughest problem was the health of the animals: both drugs and veterinarians were increasingly in short supply. Dad and I had always turned to prayer first when disease threatened our herds; now it was often both first and last defence.

Throughout the war years, Rose and I continued to sponsor summer tent meetings, following the pattern we'd worked out in East Los Angeles. Find a gifted speaker and do the thing where our gifts seemed to lie – get the churches of a certain area working together, rent equipment, handle details. Then, when some of the major expenses had been met, put any additional offering money into a bank account administered jointly by the churches involved, so that when the meetings ended, the co-operation wouldn't.

At our own church some of the Elders still wondered aloud what we were getting out of "all this rushing about." But when Florence walked without a trace of a limp to the front of a meeting in July 1942, and sang the glorious opening anthem, Rose and I knew that all the effort of all our lives could not express enough gratitude to God.

That was another source of joy during these years – the deepening friendship with Charles Price. I loved to hear him preach in the eloquent style he had perfected under William Jennings Bryan. Better yet were the person-to-person visits. Almost every week from 1941 to 1946 he'd come to Downey and we'd go to his favourite Italian restaurant. We'd take a booth in the back, and I'd spend the afternoon listening to the wisest man I have ever known.

"Dr. Price," I said one time, "it must be the most wonderful thing in the world to do what you do! To see thousands swayed by your words – to see people saved and healed and feel the power of God moving through you!"

Dr. Price stopped twisting spaghetti on his fork and fixed me with a strange little frown.

"It isn't like that," he said at last. "It's . . . like this war." He waved an arm around the room; we were almost the only civilians in the place. "Where are soldiers getting killed? In the front lines, where they're closest to the enemy.

"Demos, it's the same way with evangelism. This is a war,

as deadly as what's happening on Guadalcanal. A preacher who carries the attack into enemy territory comes under fire. He gets hurt, Demos. Some of us are destroyed."

He gave the self-deprecating little laugh so characteristic of him. "Sometimes people try to compliment me, tell me what a fluent speaker I am. That doesn't mean a thing to me. But last evening a lady told me her family prays for me every day. Demos, that's the most wonderful thing any preacher can hear."

I nodded my head, impressed with his earnestness. But the reality of what he was saying, back in the early forties, I did not understand at all.

It happened almost unnoticed in the pressures of wartime red tape and shortages. Dad's original three cows had become three thousand; we were the largest private dairy in the world.

And had the largest private headache, I would think, as I hung on the phone hour after hour, tracing a rumour that there were milk bottles available here, cement for a dairy floor there. Just getting enough food for such a number of animals was increasingly difficult. I was now driving all the way out to the Imperial Valley to buy hay.

Most of this trip led through the desert and, as a sweltering July gave way to an even hotter August 1943, an amazing change came over the once-lonely road. Where a couple of sun-parched shacks had been on my last trip, there would be a bustling tent city on my next, traffic slowing to a crawl behind convoys of army trucks. All the way along the route it was the same – date farms and dusty hamlets suddenly bursting at the seams with soldiers. Nobody said anything of course, nobody knew anything, but it was obvious that a great desert campaign was in the making somewhere on the face of the troubled earth.

I would talk about it to Rose when I returned home. "So many boys, Rose, and they look so hot and bored."

The town of Indio, twenty-five miles east of Palm Springs, haunted me particularly. The streets were so jammed with off-duty soldiers that it took an hour just to drive through. I would sit in the standstill traffic and watch them, waiting in endless lines at the three or four small restaurants and the single theatre – seeking a little shade against the 120° heat. Nothing to do and nowhere to go.

And I thought: What if we were to bring a tent meeting here!

"More meetings, Demos?" asked Dad. Rose and I had just finished sponsoring a six-weeks' revival in Orange County.

Rose, too, was doubtful. "Demos, you're working sixteen hours a day at the dairy. During the revival you scarcely got to bed at all. What will you prove by killing yourself?"

"But if this idea comes from God, Rose, and not from me?"

She looked up from the sunsuit she was ironing. "Then we'll do it."

I jumped up from the sofa. "I'll phone Charles Price right away," I said. "He's pretty well booked ahead but maybe he'd have a week or two free."

Rose lifted another of Gerry's playsuits from the heap of sprinkled clothes. She was never one to talk a lot but whenever she had absolutely nothing to say, I knew that she had the most to tell me.

"Rose?"

Silence.

"Is something wrong?"

"Demos, as much as I love and respect Dr. Price, he's wrong for talking with soldiers. We need someone younger, someone . . . I don't know. Someone who can play a guitar."

I was sure Rose was wrong. "Look at the crowds Dr.

Price draws," I said. "Look at the healings that take place. Look at Florence."

Rose was silent again. And so I called Charles Price, forgetting the very lesson I had learned back when we started holding meetings in Lincoln Park: for Rose and me the key to finding God's will was agreement.

Dr. Price was sympathetic to the situation of the soldiers out in the desert, and said he would try to rearrange his commitments. He did, too, I think, though a raise just then in our milk quota kept me preoccupied for a while. But then Dr. Price got the flu and I had difficulty finding the military authority who could give permission for such meetings, and by the time Dr. Price's doctor told him absolutely he could not do it, the urgency I had felt about the situation had passed. I had missed God's moment or God's man for this particular job. I made a few half-hearted attempts to find someone else to lead some meetings, and in the end did nothing at all. . . .

That fall the newspapers were full of stories from the war. American deaths were high. Each time new figures were released, the agonising questions returned. How many of the young men I had driven past, here in the California desert, were among the casualties? How many might have come to meetings in Indio? How many might have discovered the truth that would have meant everything to them?

And meanwhile there was another anxiety. All over Southern California dairymen faced a crisis. With so many veterinarians away in the service, tuberculosis was on the rise in cattle. Every thirty days officials from the state and county health departments arrived to test our herds. The injection was made in the smooth, hairless skin at the root of the cow's tail. If the skin remained smooth after three days, the animal was uninfected. But if a bump the size of a pencil eraser appeared she was classed as a "reactor"; a smaller bump made her "suspect." When incidence of reactors and suspects in any herd reached a certain level, all the animals had by law to be destroyed, unaffected ones as well as sick ones.

Several herds in neighbouring counties had already been slaughtered when the first of our cows showed up with the disease. Of course Dad and I prayed over them. Nine-year-old Richard prayed for them when he came to help out in the barns after school. It was Reliance Number Three, our model dairy, where the problem was. Nearly one hundred animals there now tested as reactors, with two hundred suspects. If there was any increase at all in these figures on the inspector's next visit — as seemed inevitable — all one thousand cows must be destroyed.

The day we received this news Dad and I remained on at Number Three long after the evening milking, sitting disconsolately at our two facing desks. No dairy we'd ever heard of had reached this incidence of disease and saved their herd.

To cheer us up Dad switched on the nightly radio broadcast from Angelus Temple. Into the gloom-filled room came the warm voice of Dr. Kelso Glover. Dr. Glover was speaking that night about God's power to heal any and every disease. Dad's eyes met mine across the desks.

Early the next morning I telephoned Dr. Glover. "When you said 'any disease,' sir, did that include sickness in cows, too?"

There was a long silence over the phone as the Berkeley trained theologian thought this over. "Any disease," he repeated finally. "In animals or men."

"Then, sir, would you be willing to pray for one thousand Holsteins? Today?" And I described the situation at Reliance Number Three.

He arrived at the dairy at 11.30 A.M. and the two of us went out to the corrals. There were sixty animals in each enclosure, most of them with their heads in the hay mangers at the farther end. But as Dr. Glover and I stepped through the first gate they stopped eating and crowded around us, as cows will, in a gently jostling circle.

Although the sun was directly overhead Dr. Glover removed his hat; I snatched off mine as well. "Lord Jesus!" he cried. "The cattle on a thousand hills are Yours! In Your Name, Lord we take authority over every tuberculosis germ attacking Your creatures."

The cows' ears pricked up; their moist black eyes regarded him earnestly.

It took three hours to visit every one of the corrals. I worried about the sun for Dr. Glover was not a young man, but he would not replace his hat so long as he was praying – and indeed the atmosphere out there among the silos and watering troughs had grown strangely hushed.

The hands sensed it too. They were mostly old-timers, men too old for the armed services and the factories, who'd been with Dad and me many years and were used to Pentecostal goings-on. But I could see that Glover's manner impressed them. When he rebuked disease you could almost see the germs turn and flee.

Now I could hardly wait for the next lesion test. But it went just as usual, the health officers' faces grim and preoccupied as they went up and down the rows of cows – tests were done in the milking barn while the animals were in their stanchions – pausing after each injection only to wipe their syringes with alcohol. These men knew better than most how devastating was the current epidemic.

Three days later they were back for the all-important reaction reading, two doctors from the state and the head county man. They didn't talk much as they pulled on their rubber boots. This was the toughest part of their job – telling a farmer his herd was condemned.

We milked 120 cows at once at Reliance Number Three, in thirty-stanchion rows. At the end of the first two rows the two state men met. I stepped closer to hear over the clank of the milking machines.

"It's a freak thing," said one of them. "There wasn't one reactor in that whole row. No suspects, either."

The other man blinked a little. "Not in the row I checked either!"

In that entire barnful of 120 cows, not one showed a trace of the disease. By the time the second shift had been milked and 240 cows tested tuberculin negative, the hands began to gather in the barn too. The third shift: same result.

By the end of the morning over one thousand cows had been milked and not one case of tuberculosis – or the suspicion of one – had been found, even among the animals which had previously tested active. The government men told us there was no medical explanation or precedent for such an occurrence. The only answer was the one I shared with the now-crowded barn: Dr. Glover had prayed and God had answered.

Nor did He answer only for this wartime emergency. For the rest of the time we had a dairy on this site, over twenty years, until Downey became so built up we had to move all the dairies north of Los Angeles, there was never a single case of tuberculosis, or suspected tuberculosis, at Reliance Number Three.

I think my mother was the most excited of all when Rose and I discovered we were going to have another baby, due in November, 1944. Gerry had started kindergarten and our two houses on their adjoining plots of land were too quiet to suit Mother. She had other grandchildren, of course, but my sisters and their families all lived a mile or more away – by Armenian standards practically out of touch.

And there was a special reason she welcomed our news. At forty-seven, Mother had inoperable cancer. Prayer, so effective at the dairy, had been powerless here at home. "But I'll see your second daughter, Demos!" she'd say happily. It was simply assumed in the family that the new baby would be a girl; as far back as records went there had never been more than one son in each generation of Shakarians. Mother started at once sewing tiny pink dresses and ruffled bonnets.

It was that summer, 1944, at the meetings, that I first put my finger on something that up till now had only nagged at the back of my mind. I was sitting on the platform as the evangelist spoke, gazing out over the jammed-packed tent. Pastel dresses, flowered dresses — many of the men were in uniform — some of the women, too. Women. . . .

I realized my mind had wandered from the sermon and with an effort pulled it back. But during the singing of the next hymn I scanned the audience again. Was it my imagination or were there ten women present for every man? The next night Rose counted with me. There were fourteen chairs to a row, then an aisle, in accordance with the fire regulations of Los Angeles County. I took the far right-hand section. In the first row: eight women, two men. In the third row: fourteen women.

For three successive nights Rose and I divided up the tent and counted the people. No question about it: women outnumbered men more than ten to one.

I was thunderstruck. In the Armenian Pentecostal Church, since everybody in a family attended, the numbers of men and women were always more or less equal. Here in the tent everyone sat so mixed together, with no division by sex or age, that I hadn't till now focused on this phenomenon. But then — where were these husbands and brothers and fathers?

87

"I'd never realized," I said to Charles Price over lasagna that week, "how few men are left in this area. All overseas, I guess."

Dr. Price peered at me through his round rimless spectacles.

"Demos, Los Angeles has never been so full of men! Soldiers from every state in the Union. Tens of thousands of men in defence work."

"Then – then why are there so many more women at our tent meetings?"

Dr. Price threw back his head and laughed till a group of marines in the booth across the way turned to stare. "Bless your innocent Armenian heart!" he said. "There are always more women at this sort of thing! Most American men consider religion ... I don't know ... sissy. Something for women and children. Have you ever heard of a *men's* missionary society? A *men's* Bible group? Women *are* the church in America, Demos. Except for professional clergy, of course, like me. But all the volunteer work, all the enthusiasm, all the life – it's the women."

For nights Charles' words kept me awake, tossing in bed until Rose, who needed extra sleep just now, asked me to move to the living-room sofa. That women should love and serve God I was accustomed to. The Armenian Church had always had its prophetesses. But men were the prime movers – the Elders, the Bible students, the teachers, the ones responsible for the religious training of the children. How could American men, so vigorous and successful in other ways, have given up this highest calling of all? Try as I would, I could not understand.

On November 1, 1944, our second little girl was born, a dark-haired little cherub with curling black lashes so long they brushed her cheeks. Of course every baby is special, but there was something about this one that had even the hard-to-impress nurses hanging around the nursery window at Downey Hospital.

We named her Carolyn. When Rose and I with Richard and Gerry beside us carried her to the front of the church on Goodrich Boulevard and knelt on the little rug for the traditional blessing of infants, I believed I would burst with pride in my family.

But of course from the beginning, Carolyn was Mother's special baby. Mother was finding it increasingly difficult to walk, even the few steps between her house and ours. And so Rose took Carolyn over there several times a day, and it was Mother who discovered one by one her remarkable abilities: how early she smiled, how soon she rolled over, how young she sat up. Mother even claimed that from four months on she'd distinctly said, "Zarouhi," but nobody else ever managed to hear this marvel.

That winter at our weekly get-togethers, Charles Price and I talked often about the phenomenon he had opened my eyes to – the resistance of American men to religion. I told him something else I'd noticed in our own church.

"When a man's business starts to succeed, Dr. Price, he'll stop coming to church. I've seen it over and over."

Many a time, I told him, I'd see the whole congregation down on its knees when a store mortgage was due, or a man needed a loan at the bank. But when that same man's business begins to thrive, the church that has struggled with him through the hard times suddenly doesn't see him any more. "Why should that be?"

Dr. Price leaned back against the wooden partition. "I know the answer the churches give. Worldly success versus the life of the Spirit. God and mammon – all that. But it doesn't satisfy me." He ran a hand through his thinning sand-colored hair. "What answers does the church have for men – women too – facing the really horrendous complexities of modern business? People with tremendous responsibilities, where hundreds of jobs depend on the decisions they make. I've had men like that come to me, Demos, and frankly I couldn't even understand their questions. What do I know about labour contracts and price freezes? I've had no experience in business.

"Sure, we clergy can give comfort and counsel to a man who's down and out, but what about the man who makes it? He needs God just as much, and ministers like me don't even know the language."

Other times our conversation was more cheerful. "Demos," Dr. Price said one day, "you're about to witness one of the major events foretold in the Bible. 'And it shall come to pass afterward, that I will pour out my spirit upon all flesh. . . .' It will happen in your lifetime, Demos, and you'll play a part in it."

I was always startled by Dr. Price's way of stating prophecy. In my church tradition a prophetic utterance was a very special movement of God, straightening a man's shoulders, raising his voice, spreading a solemn hush through all who heard. But Dr. Price would make the most astounding statements in the same voice in which he asked for the salt.

"The only part I'd ever play, Dr. Price, would be to sponsor an evangelist like you."

He shook his head. "It won't happen like that. Not through professional preachers. 'All flesh,' that's what Isaiah tells us. This is going to happen spontaneously – all over the world – to ordinary men and women – people in shops and offices and factories. I won't live long enough to see it, but you will. And, Demos, when you see it you'll know that the time of Jesus' Coming is very near."

Dr. Price spoke often of Jesus' return to earth these days. He talked about his own approaching death, too, though he was only sixty-two. I started to protest but he raised a hand to silence me. "Let's not be sentimental, good friend. There are simply things which I know. I have another year, more or less. And then, Demos, what a privilege for a Christian to go to his Lord!"

We never knew how Carolyn caught the flu, except that there was a lot of it in Los Angeles that March 1945.

Dr. Haygood was no longer living. Dr. Steere, who had taken over his practice, assured us she was getting better care at home than he could provide at the hospital with its wartime shortages of staff and equipment.

But around-the-clock care produced no improvement. The infection seemed to have settled in her chest; she began to breathe in gasps. When she was admitted to the hospital on the evening of March 21, the diagnosis was simple and terrible:

Pneumonia. Both lungs.

Rose never left the hospital room during the next twelve hours; I left only to make phone calls to the people whose prayers we needed. The family prayed. The church prayed. Charles Price came to the hospital room, and we tried to build our faith by remembering what God had done for Florence not many rooms away on this same corridor. But this time Dr. Price did not speak of a sensation of warmth on his shoulders, and when he left the room his face was grey.

It all happened with such stunning swiftness. At 7:00 A.M. on March 22 I was home taking a shower when the telephone rang. It was a nurse. Could I get back to the hospital? But I knew before I ever got there that our baby was gone.

And in another way it was weeks – months – before I knew. Carolyn, at almost-five-months so bubblingly alive, how could so much brightness and sparkle simply be snuffed out? We saw her for the last time in the funeral home, lying impossibly still in the small white coffin, her long lashes curled down on her round little cheeks.

At home, of course, family was already arriving, overflowing our house and the big one next door, sitting with us through the long evenings, acting out the age-old sacrament of family oneness and continuity. After the trip to the cemetery there was the sit-down dinner at church, the set speeches of condolence, which the heart stores until the mind can take them in.

But strangely enough the greatest help that first week came from two strangers. They were ladies in their mid-thirties who lived in Pasadena and drove with Charles Price to our house one afternoon. They wanted to wait outside in the car, but Rose insisted they come in. After a while Dr. Price drew me into the hallway.

"I know these women very well," he told me. "They have the rare and wonderful faculty of being able to sense the invisible angelic host which the Bible tells us sometimes visits the earth." From the moment they entered our house, Dr. Price said, the two women, Dorothy Doane and Allene Brumbach, had been aware of a vast company of angels — more than they'd ever encountered in one place. "They say the air is thronged with them."

It was a gift which got us through many bad moments.

But the bad moments came so unexpectedly! One Sunday in church Rose jumped up from her bench in the women's section and rushed out the back door. When I reached her on the sidewalk she was sobbing.

"That little baby!" was all she could say.

Then I realized that the girl sitting next to her had been holding a baby about Carolyn's age. Four young women in the church had had babies at about the time Carolyn was born, and for months the sight of these children brought the emptiness flooding back.

And yet ... as time passed we began to notice a difference in ourselves. It was as though the visible, material world around us were somehow less ... less convincing than it had been. The war was over, it should have been time to start our new home. For years we'd been planning to build a larger place, when building materials were available again. I wanted a room where I could work, Rose wanted a larger kitchen, certainly we needed a guest room for the evangelists who often spent weeks on end with us. As it was, either Richard or Gerry had to move out to the sofa.

But somehow without saying a word both Rose and I knew we were never going to build that house. Partly it was because this little house was filled with Carolyn: the corner where her crib had been, the place in the hall outside the bathroom where her bathinette had stood. But also it was that ... well, having a study and a nice neat guest room and all the new kitchen appliances no longer seemed to matter one way or another. A part of us was in heaven and from that time on, earth had a different, less urgent, look about it.

We noticed something else. In the morning after Richard and Gerry went off to school, Rose and I had always remained at the little dinette table for our morning prayer time, bowing our heads, talking to God about the concerns of the day.

Now all at once the dinette wasn't right. Again without saying a word, both of us knew we wanted to get down on our knees when we spoke to God. Together one morning we walked into the living room and knelt on the oriental rug which had been a tenth anniversary present from Rose's family. From then on this dark red carpet with its field of blue flowers was our meeting place with God. It was not that we were fearful of Him after Carolyn's death. It was that He was somehow larger, nearer, more real; His living Presence drove us to our knees with awe.

And it was in the living room one morning that I took the step I had resisted so long. "Lord," I said, "I don't know how it is with Rose, but I know I've never really put You first in my life. Oh, some tent meetings. Some of my time. Some of my money. But You know and I know that my family has been first in my heart. Lord, I want You to be first."

I felt Rose's hand in mine. It was all the confirmation I needed. Rose never was one to say a lot.

6

Hollywood Bowl

On the surface there was nothing very different about the idea. It was what we'd been doing all along, only on a larger scale. It had worked so well, the different Pentecostal churches of an area getting together. What if all the Pentecostals of the entire Los Angeles region – some three hundred churches – were to rent the Hollywood Bowl for one really gigantic meeting? Because the Bowl was so well known, people might come to such a rally who wouldn't go near a tent meeting.

The problem, as the pastors and I began to discuss it, was as usual – money. The deposit just to reserve the Bowl for a Monday night was $2,500. Advance payment on radio advertisements, leaflets and posters I figured would run $3,000 – making $5,500 just to start with, before we added lighting, parking attendants, and all the rest. Where was such a sum to come from? Certainly not from the pastors, most of whom were badly underpaid.

But – what about businessmen in their congregations? And then an idea came to me that was pure Armenian. "If I provided a chicken dinner," I asked the pastors, "could you supply a hundred businessmen to come to it?" After all, every Armenian knew that the most important things in life took place around the dinner table.

Most of them were doubtful. "We don't get a great many men at our services, Demos," — echoing what I knew so well. "Not the successful ones, anyway."

But eventually we came up with the names of one hundred men and invited them and their wives to a chicken dinner at Knott's Berry Farm.

When the evening came, the main dining room at the Farm was filled. Rose and I sat at the head table where we could look out over the others. And as I did, an extraordinary idea came to me. What if a few of these men, half a dozen, say, were to come up here and tell the rest of us why they went to church at a time when most men — especially successful businessmen — didn't. What excited them about Jesus enough to give up their one day of rest. What the Holy Spirit meant, personally, in their lives. It could be a tremendous encouragement to us all.

The next moment I blinked. Three tables away the face of a tall middle-aged man in a pin-striped suit suddenly lit up as though a spotlight had shone on it. I looked at Rose, but apparently she didn't see it. How could she miss it! The strange radiance danced and glittered around him in the crowded room and I knew this was the man I was to call on first.

Now I couldn't wait for the meal to be over. The coffee and boysenberry pie were simply frustrations, so eager was I to hear what this man must know.

At last the coffee beakers stopped circulating. Waitresses cleared away the plates, chairs were pushed back, everyone settled back to hear my appeal for money. Instead, I turned to the man in the pin-striped suit.

"Sir . . . yes, that's right . . . you there with the blue tie and that God-sent smile. Would you please come up here?" The man looked startled, but he inched his way among the tables until he was standing beside me. "Won't you share with all of us the wonderful thing the Lord has done for you?" I said.

The man shook his head in bewilderment. "I don't know who told you," he said, "but yes . . . my wife and I have so much to be thankful for!" And he went on to tell how his wife's father had recently been healed by prayer of what doctors had called terminal cancer. In the electric hush which followed I looked around the room again. Near the window another face was illuminated. "Sir, will you come here where we can all see you. . .?"

So it went for an hour and a half, one man after another in the large room would seem to me to be flooded with a kind of visible power. We heard stories of marriages healed, alcoholism overcome, business partners reconciled. I kept thinking of Charles Price's phrase *the full gospel* – for every aspect of the good news was related that evening in terms of actual experience. Brief, pithy, factual, these were the statements of practical men. No one preached, no one used fancy language, yet the combined effect was more powerful than any sermon I had ever heard.

When ten or eleven men had spoken I took the microphone again. "Friends, we've just heard the full gospel," I said, "as recounted by a group of businessmen." *Full gospel . . . businessmen.* Something in the phrase stuck in my mind.

"Don't you wish," I went on, "that more men in the Los Angeles area had stories like these to tell? Don't you wish every man, woman, and child in California knew God's power the way these men do? What better place could there be to tell them about Him than the Hollywood Bowl?"

That was literally all I had time to say. Everywhere around the room men were getting to their feet, dipping into their pockets, coming forward to place money on the table. They brought bills – ten-dollar bills, twenty-dollar bills – and checks. Checks scrawled in haste at the tables, checks written standing in the lengthening line that waited to reach the front of the room. When we added up the money at the end of the evening, the total was a staggering $6,200.

But impressive as such a figure was to me, I knew that something more important had happened that night. An idea had been born, a pattern shown, though I had not yet grasped the implications.

"Just think," I said to Rose as we drove home to Downey, "how many more businessmen there are in the world than preachers. If businessmen should ever start to spread the gospel. . . "

Afterwards, officials told us the Hollywood Bowl had never before been filled on a Monday night. For our Full Gospel Rally all 20,000 seats were taken with 2,500 people standing around the rim. That was the first night we used the candle-lighting ceremony. One lone candle, the idea is, can barely be seen in the dark. But when everyone lights his candle — when each of us uses what God has given — the blaze turns night into day.

For me it proved to be a moment of light indeed — the moment when at last I had the answer to the question I had asked as a boy of thirteen: Lord, what is the special work You have for me? I was wondering about it as I often did, while the floodlights were turned out, and the great outdoor arena was plunged into darkness. I had not become a preacher — I remained as bumbling and as awkward as ever in front of an audience. I was not a prophet like Charles Price. I was not a teacher or an evangelist or a healer. . . .

Somewhere above us a trumpet blew, the scalp-tingling sound echoing and re-echoing from the dark hills. Pinpricks of light appeared as candles were lit. The glow grew as the flame spread from neighbour to neighbour. And suddenly the Bowl leapt into light as thousands of tiny fires burned together.

A helper. It was as though the word were written in the twinkling flames themselves. A passer-on of what one man has to the next man. A provider of time or place or occasion for candles to come together. An encourager of the spark that could set the world on fire.

The excitement of it made tears stand in my eyes. Later that night, at home, I turned eagerly in my Bible to First Corinthians 12:28. How often I had pondered and prayed over this list of divine appointments: "... first apostles, second prophets, third teachers, then workers of miracles, then healers ..." Yes! There it was: "... helpers. ..." How had I missed this word standing there honourably among the rest? "Healers, *helpers*, administrators, speakers in various kinds of tongues."

Here was my job – the work assigned to me by God Himself – revealed in a flash of light among the Hollywood hills. God had called me – me! – to be a helper, and from that moment on the wonder of my appointment would never leave me.

It was good that I had this encouragement, for shortly afterwards came an experience that might otherwise have soured forever the joy of helping. The speaker at one of our many meetings was an evangelist from the East. He came on what appeared to be the highest recommendations. But he did seem an odd figure for an evangelist with his bush of silver shoulder-length hair and that artificial leg of his! From the first it seemed to me that he took an unusual interest in the offering money, frequently commenting that in other places the collections would go directly to him.

"They would here, too," I said, "if you were holding your own meetings." When an evangelist had his own organisation, I reminded him, with staff salaries to pay, publicity, travel, and lodging – of course he counted on the offering money to make all this possible. In that case, it was the evangelist himself who rented land, hired construction crews.

When we sponsored the meetings, on the other hand, the evangelist had none of these concerns, not even his own living expenses, because he stayed in our house and ate Rose's good home-cooked meals. Rose and I, I told him, spent hundreds of dollars on each campaign that we never expected or wanted back. After major expenses had been met, all offering money went to the churches.

With one exception. Once a week we took up what we called a "love offering," a collection for the evangelist's own needs. It had been our experience that at the end of the six weeks' campaign he'd have enough to finance his next series of meetings on his own.

As I say, I went into it in such great detail with him, because I could see that the subject was on his mind. But even after this explanation, he continued to ask at the close of each service what the receipts had been. "You could get a lot more than that," he'd say. "You don't pitch it right. You have to tug on the heartstrings, if you want people to give."

"We *don't* want them to give," Rose said across the supper table, passing him the meatballs for the third time. "Not because *we* ask them to. If the Holy Spirit tells them to give, that's different. And He'll specify the amount."

The strange thing about the fellow was that in spite of his over-concern for money, he was an anointed, God-inspired speaker. We never had bigger crowds than we had that summer, never more people coming forward to the altar, never more wonderful healings. One night a deaf child heard for the first time in his life. At the end of the week his doctor testified to his healing from the platform. Another night a woman was relieved of a tremendous disfiguring goitre.

At last it was the final Sunday afternoon. Over ten

thousand people jammed the huge tent as Bob Smith (not his real name) gave the stirring closing sermon. He was truly a gifted speaker, I thought, and I was glad for his sake that the meetings had been financially successful, too, the poor fellow seemed to have such anxiety about the subject. He'd received enough in the love offerings to finance several campaigns back East, or wherever he chose to go.

My eyes drifted along the rows of spectators. Still overwhelmingly female, I saw. What was the answer to making God real and alive for men today?

". . . God's richest blessings," Smith was saying. My mind returned with a jerk to the sermon. "He cannot give to you unless you first give to Him. Empty your purses, friends, that He may fill you with all the riches of heaven!"

What was the man talking about purses for? There wasn't to be a collection at all at this final service.

"Who will give?" he persisted. "Give sacrificially, give until God's hands are untied to give to you?"

A woman in a pink dress was coming down the aisle toward the platform. Smith stepped out from behind the pulpit and leaned down through the potted plants to accept what she held up to him.

"Bless you, sister!" he cried. "God will bless you mightily for this deed of love!" Here and there under the huge canvas others were starting down the aisles. I got up from my chair at the rear of the platform and let myself over the side. There behind the stage a little cluster of ushers and local pastors was forming.

"What does he think he's doing?" Rose's brother Edward Gabriel asked. (Rose's family had recently shortened their name from Gabrielian to Gabriel). "He has no right to do this!"

"We've got to stop him!" I agreed.

But how? The emotion of the people responding was real,

even if the preacher's was not. He was weeping now, as he
gathered in the offerings: "Thank you, brother!" "God will
reward you, sister!" "God bless you ... and you ... and
you. ..."

What could we do? These people had heard the word of
God preached for weeks by this man, seen healing per-
formed here. Many had given their lives to Christ as a result.
By exposing him, would we undermine their faith?

'But we'll make good and sure he doesn't walk out of here
with these people's money," said Edward. Edward was head
usher for the meetings.

The unblushing appeal went on. Gerry grew restless with
sitting so long, and Rose took the car keys and drove her
home. When Rose got back – a thirty-two mile round trip –
the man was incredibly still at it. He was making it a point of
public witness to come forward "in the sight of all" and "be
counted" as one who loved God. To return a second and even
a third time was an even greater demonstration of devotion.

For an unbelievable two and a half hours, long after the
scheduled close of the meeting, the collection went on. Here
and there in the audience I saw faces looking as bewildered
as I felt; perhaps four hundred people had left. But most of
the congregation seemed utterly enraptured by his perfor-
mance. Sometimes it seemed that the entire tent was on its
feet at once, surging forward to place their money in the
offering buckets at the evangelist's feet.

At last when there could scarcely have been a dollar bill
left in a pocket or a purse, he bowed his head for the closing
prayer. As swiftly as a military manoeuvre Edward and his
team of ushers closed in on the platform. Before Smith could
protest they had scooped up the buckets and headed toward
the rear of the platform.

"You men – ah, brothers!" Smith stammered. "I'm – I was
blessing these gifts!"

"Amen!" the ushers echoed, and vanished into the curtained-off area we used as a backstage office.

We were in this office alcove a few minutes later, beginning to count the money when Smith burst through the flaps, the veins on his temples pulsing with rage.

"That's mine!" he said. "All of that's mine!"

He had an old soft-sided leather satchel with him which he slammed onto the table. I'd never seen it before; certainly he had not had it in the car when he and Rose and I had driven from Downey this afternoon. He jerked the case open and began stuffing it with the bills that lay on the table.

Edward seized a handle of the satchel while another man grabbed Smith's arm.

"Don't touch him!"

It was my own voice saying it. "Don't lay a finger on that man!"

The ushers stared at me uncomprehending. I was just as dumbfounded as they were. For all at once I seemed to be looking, not at a very flushed, very angry preacher, but at Saul, King of Israel, and hearing words out of the Bible:

". . . who can stretch forth his hand against the Lord's anointed . . .?" (1 Samuel 26:9).

Those were David's words, I remembered, and he had spoken them about Saul, *after* Saul had turned away from God, disobeyed Him, was actively fighting against Him. Still Saul remained in David's eyes the man through whom God's power and blessing had flowed – as I had seen them flow through Bob Smith.

Smith was stuffing bills into the bag as fast as his hands could move.

"Demos!" Edward said, "Do you see what he's doing!"

"I see."

"And you're going to let him walk off with that money?"

"Why shouldn't I?" said Smith. "It's mine, isn't it?" He

103

was holding the satchel below the table now, sweeping the money into it with his arm.

"Yes, Bob, it's yours," I agreed, still scarcely believing my own voice. "God doesn't supply His money by these methods."

"Methods!" Smith shot back scornfully. "You don't know anything about methods. You're a fool, Shakarian. You're all of you fools!" He snapped the bag shut and stood glaring at the little circle of laymen and pastors. "You have a fantastic thing going here and you don't even know it!"

He backed toward the door, feeling behind him for the break in the curtain. The next moment he was gone.

I had to put both hands on Edward's shoulders to keep him from chasing after him. "Let him alone!" I repeated. "What could we do with that money? It's not of God, and I don't believe God will bless it."

Once more I had the sense of voicing words that did not originate with me. Then the moment passed and a great weariness settled over me – weariness of people, of meetings, of tents, of platforms and loudspeakers. We stepped out into the huge canvas arena. The crowd was still inching up the aisles toward the exits; volunteer teams from the churches were stacking the rows of folding chairs. There was no sign of Bob Smith.

I found Rose and told her to go on home. It would be hours yet before I was through for the night. There was the cleanup to organize, the knockdown crew to drive out from town. Tomorrow I'd be back to get the landscapers started. And I was so sick of it, so terribly sick of it. . . .

In Richard's room at home there was no trace of the man who had lived there for six weeks. His clothes were gone from the closet, his two blue suitcases vanished, even his toothbrush gone from the rack in the bathroom. When he had packed up none of us knew. Certainly there had been no good-by to any member of the family, no thank you to Rose for her weeks of hospitality.

It was six years before I heard another word of Bob Smith. Then one morning he himself walked into the main office at Reliance Number Three, gaunt, unshaved, shabbily dressed – to all appearances a man without a dime. He told me a long hard-luck story and asked for money to get to Detroit, which I gave him. Three years after that we heard that he had died.

This was the first – but by no means the last – time that Rose and I encountered the phenomenon of a man with a tremendous ministry of God for others, whose own personal life was a shambles. Sometimes as with Smith, the problem was money. Sometimes it was alcohol. Sometimes women, or drugs, or sexual perversion.

Why did God honour the ministry of men like this? Was it the power of Scripture, working independently of the man who quoted it? Was it the faith of the hearers? I didn't know.

Only two things I was sure of. That people who gave their hearts or their purses to God at such meetings did not lose their reward because the human agent was faulty. And that the words I had spoken without understanding them remained true.

"Don't touch him."

These men were in God's hands – I found I wasn't allowed even to speculate too much about it. Only, often, I would think of Charles Price's words, spoken with such a look of pain: "The men in the front lines get hurt." And I would think of the risks and temptations facing such men, and ask myself if I had prayed enough for Bob Smith. . . .

Charles Price was dead. He had died, as he had known he would, in 1946. But my mother, although in almost constant pain, was still alive. After Carolyn's death the family expected her to go very swiftly. Carolyn's chubby little hands gripping her thin, worn ones had seemed to be the strength that kept Mother going.

But there was one piece of unfinished business. Florence at twenty-one was still unmarried – for an Armenian mother an intolerable way to leave her earthly affairs. And so when Florence became engaged to a handsome young Armenian whose own mother had died some years before, Mother took the wedding in hand.

Her strength during those months was a source of mystery to her doctors who could not understand how she was even able to walk. She shopped, she sewed, she even cooked most of the elaborate banquet that followed the wedding ceremony.

And then when the radiant young couple had departed on their honeymoon, she went back to bed. The cancer had progressed past the point where drugs could help the pain, but I never heard Mother utter a word of complaint – only thanksgiving that she had been able to complete her family duties.

Dr. John Leary, the specialist who attended her those last months, used to come to the big Spanish house early each morning, "To start my day right," he'd tell me. He said he had a score of patients not nearly as ill as Mother whose troubles left him exhausted. "But if I can have fifteen minutes with your mother, Demos, at the start of the day, I can face anything that comes."

When she died in November 1947, at the age of fifty, I learned how many people had drawn courage from her. It was the biggest funeral Downey had ever seen. Everyone was there, from community leaders to homeless drifters – it was then that I learned the extent of Mother's hospitality.

But in many ways the most important person there was also the youngest one, sleeping unconcernedly in Rose's arms, four-month-old Stephen.

When we'd learned that we were to have another baby we knew somehow that the timing was for Mother, that she would hold this child before she died. And so she had. Long after Dr. Leary had forbidden other visitors, we would take Steve up to Mother's bedroom. And Mother would stroke his soft black curls and say — sometimes we had to bend very close to hear — "A second son ... it has never, never happened, that God would send a second son. ..."

7

The Testing Time

Dad was back in the office. The last weeks of Mother's life he'd spent most of every day in her room. Now he was back again at the desk facing mine in Reliance Number Three, his brow puckered in a frown as he read the quarterly reports.

"You're stockpiling, son," he said, pointing to figures which showed an inventory of grain greater than we needed for current demands. Dad had never been comfortable with the milling operation because of the yo-yo prices.

But that objection hardly seemed to apply in the gathering post-war boom. That winter of 1947-48 everyone dealing in commodities agreed on one point. It was only the government ceiling which was keeping grain prices down. Oats, barley, corn, cottonseed meal, soybean meal, they'd all stayed right at this arbitrary ceiling for months, as if trying to force their way through. The minute the ceiling was lifted, prices would soar. It had seemed to me good business to stock up heavily while the ceiling was on.

This is what Dad's sharp Armenian eye caught as he looked over the figures. His frown deepened as he noted that I had committed us to hundreds of thousands of dollars' worth of grain at current prices to be delivered the following fall.

In making this commitment I had lit the fuse of the bomb.

The name kept popping into my mind at the strangest moments.

Fresno.

Why should I keep thinking of Fresno? It was a city some two hundred miles north of Los Angeles that I'd driven through a number of times. But I knew nobody there and had no special connection with it. Why should Fresno suddenly be on my mind?

With the sting of the Bob Smith affair still smarting, Rose and I hadn't talked much about our next summer's plans. Someone suggested that we hold meetings again in East Los Angeles, and it seemed like a good idea.

When I got home one night Rose was in our bedroom, putting little Steve in his crib. "Honey," I said, "all the way driving home tonight the name of a particular town kept hammering at me. I can't stop thinking about it."

Rose straightened up and looked at me. "Don't say the name! The same thing's been happening to me!" She switched out the light, and we tiptoed together from the room. In the hallway she turned to me.

"It's Fresno, isn't it?"

I shook my head in wonderment.

"It's Fresno."

But if we knew *where* God wanted us to work, the next question was *how*. We had no contacts there, no knowledge of the place.

At last from a minister in L.A. I got the name of the pastor of an Assemblies of God church in Fresno. I phoned him and sounded him out about holding meetings that coming summer in his city. There was a very long silence over the phone. Finally he said he'd call me back, and a few weeks later I found myself hosting him and thirty-three other local pastors to a steak dinner at the California Hotel in Fresno. The time-tested Armenian method of feeding the body along with the soul probably accounted for the good turnout; certainly it was not enthusiasm for the project. I had never seen such suspicious faces as those that turned toward me as I rose to speak.

I described the tent meetings we'd held in Los Angeles for seven summers now, speculated on the thousands of people who knew God today because of them. Silence. Hostile stares. At last one of the men got to his feet, hitched his trousers and voiced what was apparently on everyone's mind: "What do *you* get out of this, Mr. Shakarian? What have you got up your sleeve?"

I felt a hot blush rise up my cheek — then checked myself. Why *should* these men take a total stranger at face value? I thought of Bob Smith and for the first time felt grateful for that experience. God knew I was slow-witted. Maybe the only way He could show me anything was to rub my face in it. A pastor *should* be suspicious, *had* to ask questions where the welfare of his people was concerned.

And so for the thirty-four men I went over my procedure: I took no salary, paid all my own expenses. Here in Fresno these would be higher than usual, since Rose and I would have to move up for the duration of the meetings. After the major expenses were met — advertising, erecting a tent, that kind of thing — any money received at the meetings would belong jointly to the participating churches. On the other hand, if there were a deficit I would pay it out of my own pocket.

"What do I get out of it?" I echoed. I pulled my New Testament out of my pocket and read aloud the verses in First Corinthians 12 which had come to mean so much to me. "Friends," I said, "I believe God has a particular gift for each of His servants, some special ability we're to use for His Kingdom. I believe if we find that gift — and use it — we'll be *the happiest people on earth.* And if we miss it, no matter how many excellent things we do, we'll be utterly miserable.

"I'm lucky," I said. "I've found my job. I'm a helper, like it says right here. My gift is to help other people do what *they* do best. I'll help you get together, help set up a meeting place, help you find speakers. What I'll get out of it is the joy of using the talent God gave me."

I crooked my left arm and peered into the coat sleeve. "No," I said, "nothing there. . . ."

In the burst of good-natured laughter which followed the tension broke. From everywhere around the room came suggestions for the Fresno meetings. This pastor had a contact at the local radio station, that one knew the manager of a printing press. Fall, they all agreed, would be better than summer here in Fresno – in October after the grape harvest was in. There was a large hall in the centre of town, Memorial Auditorium, which would be more comfortable than a tent.

"Sounds like a busy few months, Demos," said Floyd Hawkins, one of the pastors, as he saw me out to my car. "You'll be away from your office a lot. I sure hope the business is going okay."

I gave him a reassuring smile. "Couldn't be better, Floyd," I said. "Couldn't be better." I located an unfurnished frame house for rent on G Street only five blocks from Fresno Memorial Auditorium. Furnishing it was no problem. When the time came I'd simply load what we needed onto one of our big diesel hay rigs – chairs, tables, beds – "and the washing machine," Rose reminded me. "I couldn't face the diapers without my machine."

The house was big enough, too, so that the different evangelists could stay with us as they always did in Downey. This time a different man was to preach each week.

There'd be five weeks of meetings, Rose and I wanted to be

there a week early; afterwards there was always at least ten days' work to clear up loose ends. We decided that at nine years old it wouldn't hurt Gerry to attend school in Fresno during these weeks, but that Richard, who was in eighth grade, had better not miss his regular classes. Which was a satisfactory way of arranging what we all knew and didn't say: we couldn't all go off and leave Dad. Since Mother's death Dad's lonesomeness had been something you could almost touch. And so it was settled that Richard would stay with his grandfather, with both of them joining us on the weekends.

The final blessing seemed to be given to the project with the news that Mrs. Newman, the practical nurse who had stayed with us when each of the children came home from the hospital, would join us so that Rose could play the piano for the meetings.

And so it was with the sense that God was really in this planning that I drove out to the mill on a Monday morning in October, to finish up some last-minute affairs before leaving for Fresno next day. To my surprise our bookkeeper Maurice Brunache was standing at the front door. His face was exactly the colour of the fine flour-dust that settles over everything at the mill.

"It's happened, Demos." He had some papers in his hands.

"What's happened?"

"The price ceiling. The commodity market opened in Chicago this morning without it."

"That's great, Maurice! It's what we've been. . . ." Something in Brunache's face stopped me. I followed him silently into the office and took a chair — and it was just as well I did.

"I'm afraid it's not great, Demos."

"You mean — prices didn't change?"

"They changed, all right. They *fell*." He consulted the

paper he was holding. "On our present inventory we've lost $10,500. But deliveries are rolling in every day now. We haven't got space to store that much grain. We've got to go on selling it, and as of now every sale is costing us money."

I took the papers from Maurice's hand. The rules of the commodities market allow for a maximum price drop in any one session. Within a few minutes of today's opening, I saw, grain had hit that maximum loss. And we, of course, had to go on paying the top ceiling price I had contracted for months ago.

"This price drop isn't over yet, Demos. If the market continues to fall, you could be . . . wiped out."

In a daze I walked out of the mill. It was crazy. It made no sense. And yet it was happening. Even as I got into my automobile another boxcar of feed was rolling into the siding. Glumly I calculated how many dollars that one carload was costing me.

Next morning, Tuesday, I loaded Rose's washing machine and some furniture onto the hay truck and sent it on its way. When I got back in the house the phone was ringing.

Maurice Brunache. "It went the route again, Demos," he said. When the market opened in Chicago grain once more, against all predictions, had fallen straight to the maximum allowed by the Exchange. In less than an hour we had again lost more than ten thousand dollars.

"It's really too bad about the Fresno trip," Maurice went on. "I know how much that campaign would have meant to you."

"*Would* have meant?"

"Well, you can't very well leave now! Demos . . . are you there?"

I was there, but my mind had gone back, three and a half years, to a promise. God's business was to come first. Before the family. Before anything else in the world.

"I've got to go on, Maurice," I said. "Look, this price drop's some kind of freak. It's bound to straighten out. We'll keep in touch by phone."

But all the way to Fresno a little voice went round and round with the whine of the tires. "You'll be wiped out. You'll be wiped out. You'll lose the mill. You'll be wiped out. . . ."

I was setting up Stevie's crib in the house on G Street late that afternoon when there was a little cry from the kitchen where Rose and Mrs. Newman were putting away dishes.

"My watch!" Rose wailed from the top of the stepladder. "It's not on my arm!"

I rushed into the room and stared up at her, remembering the night I had crossed the Gabriels' living room and struggled to fasten it on her arm. "Are you sure you were wearing it?"

"Of course I'm sure! I remember looking at it as we got out of the car."

Well, we tore that kitchen apart. I even went out to the car and searched the walk between there and the house. Rose remembered unpacking some things in Gerry's bedroom too, but before we could start searching there, Mrs. Newman called us both into our room where she was putting Stevie into his pyjamas. "Feel his head," she said. "I didn't think he was himself today – fussing all the way up in the car. I'm going to take his temperature."

The three of us stood silently in the unfamiliar little room as she held the thermometer up to the blue-shaded lamp. Her eyes widened.

"A hundred and four and a half. . . ."

From one of the Fresno pastors we got the name of a doctor, but when he arrived he could only confirm the temperature reading Mrs. Newman had gotten, and tell us to continue the alcohol baths she had already started.

114

Sponge baths, ice packs, aspirin, nothing would budge that fever. By morning Steve's eyes were glazed, his skin dry to the touch. The doctor came again and wrote out a batch of prescriptions. I begged Rose to lie down for a while but she scarcely seemed to hear me.

When Steve was still no better by evening I phoned home to get Dad and the church to pray — and learned that grain had had another disastrous day on the stock exchange. Rose at last fell asleep with exhaustion, and Mrs. Newman and I took turns sitting up by the crib.

Thursday morning the planning sessions began with ushers and counsellors, but I found it hard to keep my mind on what we were doing. I kept slipping out to phone the house on G Street only to hear, "No change." "He's very flushed." "He can't seem to swallow."

For three more days it continued the same. It was terrible to see that lively little boy lying so still, only his chest shuddering with the effort of breathing. Hour after hour Rose or Mrs. Newman stood over the crib spooning water between the parched little lips.

I'd almost forgotten about the mill when on Friday afternoon Maurice Brunache phoned to say we'd lost over $50,000 during the week. Saturday came. The meetings were to start next day and Steve was no better. A local store had donated some light blue carpeting for the front of the auditorium below the stage, an enormous roll sixteen feet wide and a hundred feet long. Saturday afternoon I was over there supervising the installation, when suddenly I knew that if I didn't get away I'd start to cry.

"You don't need me for this," I mumbled to the guy from Josephine's Furniture Store. I walked quickly out to the car and simply started driving. Through the city, out into the San Joaquin Valley. In the vineyards yellow-brown grape leaves flapped mournfully against their stakes in the October wind.

"Lord Jesus, You are the Vine. We are only twigs and branches. Without You we can do nothing. Certainly I've been able to do less than nothing this week. Is it because You're not in this campaign? Have I set the whole involved business in motion without You?"

Even as I spoke a voice answered me. An inner voice, yet as unmistakable as though I heard it with my ears.

Demos, you are to abandon this Fresno campaign. You are to go back to Los Angeles where you can get proper care for your child and look after your business. You are bringing dishonour on My name with this illness and this loss.

I pulled the car to the side of the road and snapped off the engine with shaking hands. Somehow even in the midst of fear and anxiety I hadn't expected this answer. Then – all those seeming encouragements, all the answered prayer – it had all been only my own imagination.

But ... what could I do now? Surely it was too late to stop plans so far along?

That is your pride, Demos. That is only your fear of looking foolish.

At last I started up the motor and drove back to the house on G Street. Steve's fever was still one hundred and four degrees. Billy Adams had arrived, Mrs. Newman told me, our song leader from Los Angeles, and had gone over to see the auditorium. Rose was asleep in Gerry's room. I realized for the first time how exhausted I myself was. I lay down, but sleep wouldn't come.

You are to abandon the campaign. You are to return to Los Angeles.

All night I turned restlessly on the bed, listening to Steve's hard, dry little cough. I heard Billy Adams come in. Heard Rose making ice packs in the kitchen.

Your pride . . . your pride. . . .

Outside, the sky grew light. Steve began to cry, a weak, listless little whimper. Surely God would not attack a tiny child just to teach me humility? But the accusing voice continued.

Abandon the campaign. Go back to Los Angeles. You'll be wiped out. . . .

I sat bolt upright in bed. I recognized that voice! It was the one that had whispered to me in the car driving up on Tuesday. And again yesterday in the grape fields. Fear. Doubt. Confusion. Self-hate. These were not the signs of God's Presence. These were the tools of the great Deceiver.

And if he was so set against these meetings, why then, God must be for them!

"Rose! Billy!"

I raced out to the living room where Rose was walking Steve up and down. Billy Adams came out of the kitchen carrying a fresh-brewed pot of coffee.

"It was Satan!" I told them. "It was Satan trying to get us to call the whole thing off! God wants us to hold these meetings!"

Billy set the coffeepot on the glass-topped table. "Did you ever doubt it, Demos?"

And so subtle, so devastating had the attack been, that I had to confess that I had.

"But no more," I said. "We're going to go there this afternoon and we're going to praise God, and we're going to laugh in the devil's face."

And so we did, asserting God's victory even though to

the outward eye nothing at all had changed. All the five-block drive to the auditorium Rose cried at leaving Steve, although we reminded each other over and over that he was in the best possible hands with Mrs. Newman.

But when the tall curtains parted and Rose at the piano struck the first chords of the joyful opening anthem, no one in the crowd that nearly filled the big municipal hall would have guessed that she had a care in the world. Then Billy stepped to the microphone and asked the entire congregation to stand and pray for Steve's healing. We prayed, we sang, we praised God. So strong was the Spirit in the meeting that when we went home for supper between the afternoon and evening sessions, I think we all three expected Steve himself to come toddling to the door to meet us.

But there was no change. Mrs. Newman was changing his perspiration-soaked pyjamas while Gerry put a fresh sheet on the crib.

It was the same at midnight when we got back from the evening service. Fever as high as ever, eyes dull and unfocused.

And yet – and yet something was different in the small frame house. For the first time since we arrived I fell asleep as my head hit the pillow.

I was wakened in the morning by Mrs. Newman rapping on the door: "The fever's down! His temperature's normal! Oh, come and see!"

Together Mrs. Newman, Rose, Gerry, and I clustered around the crib. Steve still lay on his back, pale and tired looking, but in his large brown eyes was a hint of the old sparkle.

"Want a cookie," he said.

When we left for the afternoon meeting he was sitting up, devouring a whole box of zwieback. By the next morning there was no sign that he had ever been sick.

During his illness we'd scarcely given a thought to the business crisis, let alone something as minor as a missing watch. "But now," said Rose, Wednesday morning, "I'm going to look for that watch again! That should have told us right from the start who was behind all this trouble, Demos. It's the kind of mean, petty little trick Satan *would* pull."

All of us joined in the search, ransacking every drawer, every closet, every pocket and cuff of every piece of clothing.

No watch.

Neither was the news from the mill any more encouraging. The drop in grain prices had not been just a fluke of the market. It represented a general nationwide slump in commodity buying. Every day the mill was losing thousands of dollars.

When Dad brought Richard up that weekend he was clearly alarmed. "We can't keep this up, Demos. If we have many weeks like this last one, we'll soon be out of business."

It was Saturday morning and I was driving Dad and Richard to the Fresno County Fair. A dairyman is never so happy as when he's looking at fine cows, and I hoped it would help Dad and me forget our financial woes for a couple of hours.

Too soon it was time to go home and get ready for the afternoon meeting. At the exit to the fairgrounds, Richard stopped, fascinated by a man selling small green and brown lizards for a dollar apiece.

"Dad! Could I have. . . ."

"Don't be silly, son! Do you want to give your mother fits by bringing a slimy thing like that into the house?"

"Please, Dad! Please! They aren't slimy!" He picked one of the creatures up and stroked it gently with his forefinger. "Please, Dad!"

I stared at Richard in surprise. It was completely unlike him to insist on his own way. I was even more surprised when Dad reached into his pocket and handed him a dollar.

"Let the boy have the lizard," he scolded me.

I climbed into the car with a sigh. Dad had never been such a soft touch when I was a boy. On G Street I turned to Richard. "Now, Richard, you'll have to let that thing go in the grass. I'm not going to have a houseful of screaming women."

"Okay, Dad, but can I just show Gerry? Will you tell her to come out?"

But to my dismay it was Mrs. Newman who came. She peeked into Richard's hands, then smiled delightedly. "A chameleon!" she cried. "Oh the lovely, pretty thing! Let's find a box to keep it in!" She hurried to a pile of trash waiting at the curbside for the Saturday afternoon pickup.

A chameleon. So that's what it was. Mrs. Newman was rummaging through some discarded cartons. "That's too big. No, it needs higher sides. Here! This is just right."

She lifted the lid of a shoe box. A box that in another hour would have been bouncing along in the back of a garbage truck.

There lay the diamond wristwatch.

And so the family gained that day – besides one very popular lizard – an insight into God's care for every detail of our lives.

And as the meetings moved into their third remarkable week, with the crowds growing every night and miracles taking place on the blue carpet, I began to wonder if He would not also rescue our milling operation. Surely a floundering mill, to Him, was no bigger a problem than a missing keepsake. And without His help, we would certainly lose it. We were still paying last winter's high prices for grain, while every day we were having to sell it for less.

But the days passed and nothing changed – except for the worse. It was an extraordinary time. Every afternoon in our teaching sessions hundreds of new Christians were grounded in their new faith. Every night hundreds more came forward to give their lives to Christ, or to be healed, or to receive the Baptism in the Spirit. And every morning I spent on the telephone with grain salesmen and buyers, presiding over the loss of thousands of dollars.

It reminded me of our very first tent meeting, out on Goodrich Boulevard, when the evangelism succeeded and my fertilizer business failed. "Lord, if You tell me that these people in Fresno are more important than a feed mill, You know I can't argue. Only – I sure wish You'd told me before I ordered all this grain."

I was sitting in the kitchen of the house on G Street. It was a beautiful late October morning, all the others were out doing errands. And there in the quiet house with only the hum of the refrigerator for company, I seemed to hear a voice, weary and a little amused:

I did tell you, Demos.

I shifted uncomfortably on the hard wooden chair. Was that true? Had God from the beginning, through my father, been warning me about this situation?

For that matter, the mill itself . . . had I ever clearly heard from God that this was part of His plan for the Shakarian family? Or had it been my bright idea only? Part logic, part greed – a little empire-building, perhaps, by a man whom God had already supplied with plenty? Now when for the first time I consciously, deliberately asked Him about the milling operation, the answer came loud and clear:

It's not for you, Demos. Speculative businesses are a full-time job and I will never give you full time for any business.

Then and there I got down on my knees with my arms on the wooden chair seat. "Lord Jesus, forgive me for running out ahead of You, into a business You never called me to. Somewhere, Lord, is the man You've chosen for this work. The man who can take this business and prosper it. Send him to us now, Lord, and Lord. . . ." I looked around a little guiltily, but I was quite alone, and it was useless to hide from God what was in the heart – since He saw every grubby corner of it.

"Lord, let him offer us a good price!"

I expected Dad to be pleased with the decision to sell the mill. But when I told him about it the following weekend, he only shook his head. "How do you expect to find a buyer at a time like this? No one's going to buy into the grain business today. Why, the mill's worth less every day that passes. All anyone has to do is to wait for bankruptcy and pick it up for taxes."

"It will sell, Dad," I said, trying for his sake to sound confident. "And it will bring a fair price."

The third week of the Fresno meetings closed with a standing-room-only Sunday service. William Branham was the evangelist that week and when deaf-and-dumb twins – little boys about five years old – suddenly began to hear and to babble nonsense sounds (never having heard real language) that place broke up into rejoicing like we'd never seen.

Wednesday morning of the fourth week Dad telephoned from Los Angeles.

"Demos," he said, "you're not going to believe this but I've just had a phone call from Adolph Weinberg. He wants to buy our milling operation."

Weinberg was, like us, a Southern California farmer. He was a Jew, a devout man who had not been unduly startled to be wakened at three o'clock that morning by a voice which he recognised as God's.

Adolph, Mr. Weinberg reported the voice to have told him, *I want you to call Isaac and offer to buy their mill.*

Obedient, he had telephoned Dad. He was eager to meet and discuss terms.

"I can't get over it," Dad kept saying. "Now — of all times! How could he even have known we were selling? Did you talk to anyone but me?"

"No, Dad."

"Anyhow," Dad went on, "he's all ready to go. How soon can you get down here?"

"Dad, you know I can't leave here now."

"Why in heaven's name not?"

"Because the meetings have nearly two weeks to go. Plus the closing up after that."

"But surely the meetings can carry on a couple of days without you! It's not that important for you to be there!"

"Not to the meetings. To me. To something God's showing me. Dad, ever since these meetings started, something strange has been going on. For some reason they're a testing time for me, more than anything I've ever been through. *Who comes first?* God is asking me. Dad, I want to give Him the right answer."

"And suppose Weinberg changes his mind?"

"If he's God's buyer, he won't change it."

Almost every day for the next ten, Adolph Weinberg telephoned Dad. It seemed to him incredible that we would keep a buyer waiting, with cash in his hand, while every day the inventory in our silos dropped in value. I didn't understand it either. I only knew that Fresno was God's place for me for this moment.

The final day of the five-week campaign arrived. The Sunday afternoon meeting was scheduled to begin at two thirty. But by twelve thirty every one of the 3,500 seats in the auditorium was filled, so we began. By 2:00 P.M. there were 1,500 people standing along the walls, hundreds more waiting outside. Five o'clock came – time for the afternoon service to end. But the spirit of praise in the vast room was so powerful I could not have adjourned the meeting had I wished to.

Six o'clock. Seven. And still scarcely a soul had left the building. Most of these people had been here since before noon, and yet no one wanted to go to dinner for fear he could not get back in again.

The programme we had planned for the evening was abandoned as the Spirit took charge of the meeting. Kelso Glover was the speaker that final week, but that night he said the direction was taken completely out of his hands.

"It's like water," he told me. "Power is flowing over that carpet like water. When I step out there I feel like I'm wading clear up to my knees."

People started for the front and were healed in the aisles. One young man had arrived at the meeting in excruciating pain from an eye injury. The day before he'd been discing the ground beneath his peach trees when the exhaust pipe on his tractor tangled in a wire clothesline. Unaware of what was happening he had driven on, stretching the wire tauter and tauter until it sprang back, striking his left eye. The doctor had covered the wound with a huge airtight bandage, but made no prediction as to whether he would ever see again with that eye.

Oca Tatham came forward, he told us later, almost fainting with the pain. The instant Kelso Glover's hand touched his forehead, every trace of pain vanished, and an incredible sense of well-being flooded the injured eye.

In the sight of those 5,000 people, Tatham began to unwind the bandage. Round and round his head the layers peeled away until there was a little heap of white gauze at his feet. The innermost bandage was held on with adhesive tape. He ripped it away.

Two perfectly whole blue eyes stared incredulously from Kelso Glover to me. There was no scar, no bruise; Tatham's left eye was not even bloodshot.

It was midnight before the incredible meeting came to an end. It had lasted eleven and a half hours, yet as we drove back to the house on G Street, I felt fresher than I had that morning, and Rose and Dr. Glover said the same. I felt giddy, elated, like a man in hand-to-hand combat, who suddenly sees the enemy take to his heels. Once again I thought of Charles Price's words:

"This is a battle we're in, Demos."

Maybe the size of the victory and the bitterness of the battle were related. Maybe the enemy fights hardest where he fears the most. . . .

Now there remained only the financial loose ends to tie up, the follow-up programme to get started, the house to close. Weinberg was on the phone again.

"I'll be home next Monday, Mr. Weinberg," I promised. "You should be glad it's not sooner. Every day we wait, the price to you goes down."

"I'm offering you half a million dollars cash for a company that's losing money, and you keep stalling. I don't understand your line of thinking, Shakarian."

"Monday afternoon," I promised. And Monday at 2:00 Dad, Adolph Weinberg, and I sat down to start going over the intricate transfer of rolling mills, elevators, inventory. At the end of the first session we were $25,000 apart.

"That's my final offer," Adolph Weinberg said. "I can't go any higher."

I looked across the table at Dad. He shook his head *no*.

"And that's ours, too, Mr. Weinberg."

So the negotiations were stalled. Or so we thought. But the very next morning at 6:00 A.M. the telephone rang.

"Shakarian? Weinberg. Can you come for breakfast?"

Dad and I drove to Mr. Weinberg's house. Over scrambled eggs he told us that God had wakened him again in the middle of the night, this time with the instruction: *You are to call the Shakarians early tomorrow morning and meet their price.*

"So here I am," Adolph Weinberg said. "Your buyer. At your price. Shake hands with me, Isaac and Demos. I'd like to get a full night's sleep again."

So it was that the Lord led us through one of the most difficult times in our lives. If the attacks came from Satan, God saw to it that no genuine damage was done. Stevie came through his illness unscathed. And we were out of a business where we never belonged. Under Weinberg's management the milling operation thrived.

I had a strong feeling that God had allowed all this as preparation for some new kind of work He wanted me to do. What that work would be, I had no idea. But it would doubtless be pretty rigorous, for the training I had just completed had been very tough, indeed.

8

Clifton's Cafeteria

Ordinary men and women. People in shops and offices and factories. . . .

I could hear Charles Price's words as clearly as though he were sitting again across the lunch table: "You will witness one of the major events foretold in the Bible. Just before Jesus returns to earth, God's Spirit is going to descend on all flesh."

And laymen, Dr. Price had insisted, would be His most important channel – not the clergy or the theologians or the great gifted preachers, but men and women with ordinary jobs in the ordinary world.

When Dr. Price first began to say these things, five, six, seven years ago during the war, I scarcely listened. It seemed impossible that untrained people could have the same impact as a great evangelist like Charles Price himself.

But as the decade of the forties came to a close I found myself thinking of his words more and more often. I thought of other things: the dining room at Knott's Berry Farm when the face of one man after another had seemed to light up with the glory of God – the impact of listening to these men describe their experiences. What an irresistible force it could be if hundreds — thousands — of such men were to band together to spread this kind of Good News all over the world. . . . !

And then I would wrench my mind back again to the milk production figures in front of me.

But the idea would not let me alone. It woke me up in the night. It went with me to the office. It burned inside me as I sang the ancient Armenian melodies on Goodrich Boulevard.

All the while, of course, Rose and I were continuing to sponsor evangelists each summer. And each summer the meetings seemed more successful than the last. Why did I have this strange restlessness about them, this sense that they were no longer God's work for me? In the fall of 1951 we helped set up Oral Roberts's Los Angeles campaign, the largest yet seen in the city, with over 200 thousand attending during sixteen days. And yet. . . .

"And yet," I said to Oral one night as we sat over pie and coffee in an all-night diner after the service, "I keep getting the feeling that the Lord's showing me something different."

"What's that, Demos?"

"It's a group — a group of men. Not exceptional men. Just average business people who know the Lord and love Him, but haven't known how to show it."

"And what does this group do?"

"They tell other men, Oral. No theories. They tell what they've actually experienced of God to other men like themselves — men who might not believe what a preacher said — even someone like you — but who will listen to a plumber or a dentist or a salesman because they're plumbers and dentists and salesmen themselves."

Oral set down his coffee so hard some of it sloshed into the saucer. "Demos, I hear it. I hear it, brother! What are you going to call yourselves?"

I even knew that. "The Full Gospel Business Men's Fellowship International."

Oral stared at me across the plastic table-top. "Quite a mouthful."

"Yes, but don't you see, every one of the words is necessary." *Full Gospel.* That meant no subject would have to be avoided at our meetings. Healing. Tongues. Deliverance. Whatever the man's experience, he could talk about it, just as it happened.

Business Men. Laymen. Ordinary people.

Fellowship. That's what it should feel like. A bunch of people who love to get together — not a rules and committees and meeting-come-to-order kind of thing.

International. . . . "I know that part sounds ridiculous," I admitted. "But Oral, that's what God keeps saying to me. *International.* The whole world. All flesh." I laughed, hearing myself sounding like Charles Price.

But Oral wasn't laughing. "Demos," he said, "this is real. This has God in it. Is there anything I can do to help you get started?"

Was there! With Oral Roberts as the speaker, hundreds of Christian businessmen would turn out to an initial meeting. "Oral, if I invited businessmen from all over Los Angeles to a Saturday morning meeting, would you come and help launch this thing?"

And so it was settled. As a meeting place we chose the second floor of Clifton's Cafeteria on Broadway and Seventh, a large overflow room used at peak hours during the week but generally deserted on Saturday mornings. Then I got on the phone with every Spirit-filled businessman I knew, announcing the first meeting of the new fellowship, with Oral Roberts as the featured speaker, asking them to spread the word, to bring their friends, to help us get off to a rousing start. There was a piano in one corner of the "upper room," as I already thought of it, and Rose agreed to come and play some hymns.

The great day arrived. The traffic in downtown Los Angeles was heavy that October Saturday morning, and it took Oral, Rose and me a long time to find a parking place. We were a little late, and more than a little excited when we finally reached Clifton's Cafeteria and climbed the broad centre stairway. How many would be waiting for us upstairs? Three hundred? Four hundred?

We reached the top of the stairs. I counted quickly. Nineteen, twenty . . . twenty-one people. Including the three of us. Eighteen other men had been excited enough about the new organization to show up, even with a world-famous evangelist as an inducement.

Rose played a few hymns on the off-key little piano, but the singing reflected the lack of enthusiasm in the room. I looked around at the men who had come, most of them old friends. Dedicated people, committed Christians – and most of them already up to their eyeballs in committees and service clubs and civic organizations. The kind of men who will volunteer when a job needs doing – the kind who won't waste a minute on an outfit that isn't going anywhere.

Rose stopped playing and I stood up. I described how the conviction had grown in me that God's Spirit in the next decade would seek new channels to move in. Here and there I saw men looking at their watches. "No organs. No stained glass. Nothing that men can pigeonhole as 'religious.' Just one man telling another about Jesus."

I had never had the ability to put ideas into words, and I sat down knowing that I hadn't gotten it across.

Oral Roberts stood up. He began by thanking God for the small turnout: "So that from the beginning this will be Your organization, springing from this mustard seed of numbers, with no thanks to human know-how." He spoke for perhaps twenty minutes, and then closed with a prayer. "Shall we stand?" he said.

The handful of men straggled to their feet.

"Lord Jesus," Oral prayed, "let this Fellowship grow in Your strength alone. Send it marching in Your power across the nation. Across the world. We give You thanks right now, Lord Jesus, that we see a little group of people in a cafeteria, but that You see a thousand chapters."

With that an amazing thing happened. That little group which a minute before had been sitting around like farmhands on a fence, suddenly came alive. It was Oral's Dream of a Thousand which changed the mood. Suddenly we saw what an adventure it would be to watch the Spirit build this all-but-empty room into a worldwide army of a thousand different companies. Someone began to sing:

"Onward Christian soldiers, marching as to war. . . ."

We all picked it up: ". . . with the cross of Jesus going on before. . . ." I reached out and took the hand of the man next to me and soon we were all holding hands in a circle, marching in place, singing. The Sunday school-like simplicity of it had an odd kind of power. On and on we marched and sang. Legally the Full Gospel Business Men's Fellowship International began a few weeks later with the signing of the articles of incorporation and the naming of a five man board of directors. Spiritually, though, it began when Oral Roberts shared his Dream of a Thousand and we all held hands like children and marched in place singing a battle song.

"Rose," I said as we drove home that noon, "within a year we're going to see amazing things."

And then followed twelve months of the most incredible frustration I have ever experienced. The momentum we felt as we left Clifton's Cafeteria at once ran up against inertia and resistance.

131

We started holding breakfast meetings at Clifton's every Saturday morning. We filled our trays in the cafeteria line downstairs, then carried them to the tables upstairs for two hours of prayer and sharing. Sometimes we had a big-name speaker, but mostly we depended on the businessmen themselves. To my joy, the phenomenon I had experienced at Knott's Berry Farm was repeated: time after time I would look around the room and "know" who had an experience to share.

Yes, the meetings were all I had hoped for. It was just that there was no contagion to them, no growth. Thirty men, even forty might be there one week, fifteen the next.

And then the opposition began. What was Shakarian trying to do, pastors started asking from the pulpit, start a new denomination? Stay away from the Fellowship; they will drain men and money away from the churches.

It was the unfairness of the attack that hurt. From the beginning Rose and I had stressed two principles in every meeting we ever sponsored. "First, stay in your own church. If your church knows the power of the Spirit, go back determined to serve Him harder than ever. If not, go back a missionary.

"And second, don't leave one penny in the offering basket that belongs somewhere else. This is not where your tithe is due; your tithe belongs to your home church. Anything you give at this meeting must be above and beyond this."

We knew from years of experience that people took these points to heart. Those who attended our meetings invariably became the hardest workers and biggest givers of their home congregations. But still churches eyed the Fellowship with suspicion.

The money charge was particularly ironic; that entire year we received not a single donation. Meanwhile I was mailing out announcement letters each week, telephoning all over the country inviting men to join us when they came to Los Angeles on business. In fact, most of the time I ended up buying the breakfasts.

But a free breakfast apparently wasn't enough of a drawing card. Nothing I did was enough. And so I did more of it. I bought thirty minutes of radio time each Saturday morning and broadcast portions of the meeting to attract wider notice. I travelled all over the state, then to other western states, finally all the way to the East Coast. If people wouldn't come to us I'd go to them, describe what we were trying to do, urge them to start a group of Full Gospel Business Men in their own city.

By June I was thoroughly exhausted. After a full day's work at the dairy I was spending every evening on the Fellowship, falling into bed at three or four A.M. as weary as a man who's been swimming upstream.

And then at last it appeared we'd been thrown a lifeline. One of the speakers we invited to Clifton's Cafeteria was David duPlessis, an officer of the World Pentecostal Conference. After the meeting as we drove back out to Downey together, David could hardly contain his excitement.

"Demos," David said, "you're really on to something here. What a dream! A worldwide fellowship of ordinary businessmen filled with the Holy Spirit! Each man a missionary to the people he works with every day!"

"Thanks, David," I said gloomily, "but I'm afraid most people don't share your. . . ."

"I think," David went on, paying no attention to my mood, "that you ought to come to London next month to tell our people about this. I bet the Conference would take it on as a programme of their own."

Suddenly I was all attention. Here was a life rope, indeed, dangled over a drowning enterprise. The Pentecostal Conference represented some ten thousand churches, worldwide; if we were to tie in with them we'd no longer be a tiny group struggling on our own. We'd have sponsorship. We'd be official. David repeated his suggestion to Rose, and we eagerly agreed to come.

And ran at once into opposition from the family. Not to attending the convention – to the airplane trip en route.

"Just how do you plan to *get* to London?" my father asked when we broached the subject. We were all sitting around the Gabriels's living room one Sunday night after church. I looked at that circle of wary Armenian faces. Although this was 1952 I was the only one in the room who had ever flown – and that only in small planes for short distances.

"Gosh, Dad. By train across the country, then by boat – that would take forever. Rose is bad enough now about going away from the kids." Richard was seventeen, Gerry thirteen, little Steve almost five, and this was the first time Rose would ever have left them – and only now because Mrs. Newman was coming to stay.

"You're thinking of going in an airplane," Dad deduced after a moment's thought.

The frowns around the room deepened. "I can never understand what keeps these things up," said Aunt Siroon.

"They go awfully fast," worried Sirakan Gabriel.

"And over water," added Tiroon.

In the end it was only when we agreed to fly separately, and to sit in the very last seat in the aircraft, that the trip was given even a grudging blessing. I was to fly first, and it seemed to me that the entire congregation from Goodrich Boulevard turned up at Los Angeles International Airport to see me off. There were farewells and embraces as to a man mounting the gallows. There were promises to pray and last minute advice:

"Don't eat anything!"

"Leave your safety belt on!"

"Tilt your seat back as far as it will go!"

As the propellors whirled and caught I could see Uncle Janoian still shouting words of caution through his cupped hands.

The next day I was at New York's La Guardia Airport to meet Rose. She came down the steps beaming. She had loved her first flight so much that now she wanted to try a subway ride. We found an entrance near our hotel and rode back and forth beneath the city until everyone had gotten off except an old man with a bottle of wine in a paper bag.

Next day we were on our way to England, on separate flights in keeping with our promise to the family. But our delight at being reunited in London was dampened a little when we encountered David duPlessis.

"I'm sorry," he said, obviously embarrassed, "but I'm not getting very far with the people here. They seem to be bothered by the fact that you're a dairy farmer, not a clergyman."

"You mean they're not going to sponsor us?"

"I'm going to keep trying," was all that David would say.

Rose and I attended the public meetings of the Conference, heard the moving speeches, joined in the lively hymn singing. And at the end of the week David admitted defeat. He had not been able to persuade a single Pentecostal leader to listen to my idea.

Rose and I flew – separately – to Hamburg, Germany, with heavy hearts. "I don't understand, Lord," I prayed on the plane. "This long trip – all this time and expense – has it been for nothing? Or are You going to show me something in Germany?"

We were going to Hamburg at the urging of our friend Hal Hermann. Hal was the photographer who had made the first official pictures of the Hiroshima bomb damage for the United States government. What he saw in Japan had made him decide to devote his life to seeking God's answers for the world. We had helped him get a huge tent shipped to Hamburg, and now he wanted us to be present at his meetings.

I was met at the airport in Hamburg by Pastor Robbie, the German minister who was to be our host. "Welcome to our city!" Pastor Robbie said in excellent English. "I want to show you that our Lord is still the God of miracles." My heart raced: would this be what God had brought me so far to see?

I was astonished at how devastated Hamburg still was in July, 1952. As we drove from the airport we passed block after block of cement rubble, broken brick, and twisted trolley tracks. It seemed impossible that a soul could have lived through such destruction. At last Pastor Robbie stopped his car in front of a pile of debris indistinguishable from any other.

"This was our church," he said.

As we picked our way through brick and glass shards he added, "This is where the miracle happened."

He stopped in front of the fire-warped remains of what had once been a set of steel doors leading down into the ground. A bomb shelter, Pastor Robbie explained. "One Sunday we were in the middle of a service," he swept his arm around what had once been his church, "when the sirens blew. . . ."

Accustomed to air-raid alerts, Pastor Robbie filed his people out of the church and across the yard to the shelter. The steel doors were opened and 300 people streamed into the space below.

Then the doors were closed.

Before long an inferno of bombs exploded around them. On and on the raid went, demolishing buildings for blocks around – the church among them – fire bombs burning what remained. Down in the air-raid shelter the congregation could hear the crackling of the flames.

It seemed hours in the suffocating air of the underground room, Pastor Robbie said, before the all-clear sounded.

Eagerly he stepped up the stairs to throw open the doors. The next instant he recoiled. The metal doors were far too hot to touch. He found a piece of wood and pushed with that. The doors would not budge. Now other men were grabbing two-by-fours, pounding and hammering on the solid steel mass.

It was useless. The heat of the fire storm had fused the heavy metal together. Battering against the doors was only consuming precious oxygen.

To conserve the air as long as possible Pastor Robbie urged the people to kneel down instead and pray. "Lord," he began aloud, "we know that You are stronger than the power of death. Father, we ask You for a miracle. Open these doors, we pray, and release us."

On their knees the men and women and children waited.

After a while, far overhead, came the dreaded sound of still another airplane. Over the ruined city it flew, circling around and around. And then, the scream of a bomb. Out of instinct, as always, everyone ducked. The bomb landed close – very close. Not close enough to injure the people trapped below the ground. But just close enough to spring open the fused steel doors. As the dust settled, Pastor Robbie and his congregation filed out of the shelter into the smoking ruins above them. They stood, three hundred strong, in the light of the burning city and gave thanks to God.

That night in the Robbies' guest room I repeated the wonderful story for Rose. I felt sure there was a message in it for the problems we faced at the Fellowship. Only, I didn't know what.

Nor could I see the connection between our situation and Hal's tent meetings. It was a fascinating experience to sit in a gathering where we understood not a word of what was being said, and study the faces. Courteous and formal, this was certainly a more difficult audience than Rose and I had ever faced. I had about decided that nothing would break down German reserve when – as usual – it was a healing that changed everything. A stone-deaf man, well known to the entire city, began to hear, and that meeting went wild. People cried, they embraced, they raised their hands to heaven, just like a bunch of Armenian Pentecostals.

And still I wondered, Lord, why have You brought me here? I wasn't contributing anything, and I wasn't sure if I was learning anything. By now Rose was impatient to get back to the kids. But first she had a life-long dream to fulfil: Rose had always longed to see Venice. "And probably," we reminded each other, "we'll never be in Europe again."

And so we continued on to Italy, this time by train. What a different world rolled past the windows from the vast ranches of California! Tiny plots of land surrounded ancient stone farmhouses, while pigs, geese and chickens wandered in the yards. "Like Kara Kala!" I said to Rose. "Like the farms Dad talks about!"

In Germany I had bought a camera. Now, in spite of signs in four languages warning passengers not to lean out the window, that's what I did. I pulled down the window of our compartment and stuck head and shoulders out to get a better shot.

A searing pain knifed through my right eye.

I jerked back inside, almost dropping the camera. "Rose!"

Rose helped me to sit down, then pried my hand away from my face. My eye was quivering so that I could not open it. Rose carefully pulled up the lid.

"I can see it! It looks like a cinder. Right next to the pupil."

Rose got out her handkerchief and tried to lift the cinder out, but it was bedded too deep. The pain was agony. I pressed the handkerchief to my face to mop the stream of tears. We were still an hour out of Venice – the most excruciating hour of my life.

From the station, instead of the romantic gondola ride we

had planned we took a speedboat to our hotel. The man behind the reception desk took in the situation at a glance. A few minutes later I was stretched out on the bed in our room with the hotel doctor bending over me. He pulled back the lid, shined a flashlight on the eye, then straightened up.

"I am sorry, Signore, but we are very serious. This rock is large and he is rough."

"Can't you take it out?"

"Here? No, Signore. For this we must go to the hospital. I phone at once."

While he dialled a number and spoke rapidly in Italian, Rose sat beside me and took my hand.

"Demos," she said, "let's pray about this."

And extraordinarily enough, in my pain and disgust at myself, this was the one thing I had not done.

Rose began by thanking God for the miracles of healing we had witnessed in Hamburg. "Lord, we thank You that You are here in this room in Italy as You were present in that tent in Germany. In the name of Jesus we ask You to take away the cinder.

Even as she was speaking, a flood of warmth seemed to pass through my eye. "Rose, I can feel something! Something's happening!"

I blinked my eyes. I felt nothing. No pain. No obstruction. "Rose, look at my eye!"

Rose bent over me. "Demos, it's not there! The cinder isn't there!" She burst into tears.

The doctor hung up the telephone. "The hospital takes you. We go to the emergency room."

He took the flashlight from his bag and once again shone it into the eye. He released the lid, and examined the other eye. Then back again to the right eye.

"It is not possible," he said.

"My wife asked God to remove the cinder," I told him.

139

"It is not possible," he said again. "This rock cannot come out by himself."

"Not by itself, Doctor. God took it out."

"You don't understand. There must be a wound. A break in the tissue where he was. But there is nothing. No wound. No damage." He was backing toward the door. "I send no bill, Signore. This thing is not possible to happen. . . ."

Rose and I spent our time in Italy rejoicing.

But still — what did all this have to do with the Fellowship? When we got back to Los Angeles in late July the way ahead was no clearer than before.

August came. September. We continued to meet each Saturday morning at Clifton's Cafeteria, the same little group of men who came more out of loyalty to me, I suspected, than for any other reason. And then it was October, the first anniversary of the Full Gospel Business Men's Fellowship International. In the past twelve months I had spoken about the Fellowship in many parts of the country. Men from a number of other cities had attended our breakfasts. But in all that year that was to see such "amazing things" not one man had been impressed enough to start a second chapter in a different town.

Rose was kind enough not to remind me of my confident prediction of the previous fall, but I could see she was increasingly doubtful about the wisdom of carrying on, Saturday after Saturday. "We're just feeding people breakfast, Demos," she said. "We did a lot better with the tent meetings. We were reaching thousands every summer instead of a few dozen at best this way."

I knew she was right, yet . . . "Let's see what happens next month," I said.

But November came and went and the meetings plodded along; attendance, in fact, dropped off.

"December will be different," I assured her. "People are more open at Christmas time."

But if the Christmas season had any effect, it was to make people too busy to attend.

"I've got to take my wife shopping next Saturday, Demos."

"It's our church bazaar."

"I'm taking the kids to see Santa Claus."

Saturday morning, December 20, fifteen of us met in the upstairs room at Clifton's — six fewer than we'd started with fourteen months ago. At the close of the melancholy meeting my friend, Miner Arganbright, spoke frankly. Miner was a masonry contractor on big commercial and industrial jobs, and one of the five directors of the Fellowship.

"Demos, I hate to be negative with Christmas coming and everything," Miner said, "but I think the whole idea of the Fellowship is a dud. Frankly I wouldn't give you five cents for the whole outfit."

I stared at him, too stricken to reply.

Miner held out his hand. "You've often said this was an experiment, right?"

"Right."

"Well, lots of times experiments fail. There's no shame in that."

I still couldn't think of anything to say.

"What I'm trying to tell you, Demos, is, unless a miracle happens between now and next Saturday, you'd better count me out."

"Okay. Right, Miner. I understand."

Rose and I walked in silence down the stairs. In the big main room a Christmas tree winked on and off.

"Miner is right," Rose said softly. "If God's in something, He blesses it, doesn't He? And you just can't say the Fellowship's been blessed."

I followed her numbly onto the sidewalk. All the effort, the phone calls and travel, the virtual bribery of men to come — all for nothing. If there was one thing I'd learned since 1940 it was that when Rose and I were divided over something, the Lord was not getting through to us. If she was so sure now that the Fellowship was wrong, well — that was the end of it. The quicker I forgot about it the better.

Only ... I *couldn't* forget about it. All week long I'd find tears rising to my eyes. Driving my car to work I'd suddenly start to cry. I wondered if I was having a nervous breakdown.

For the sake of the kids, I tried to put on a bright face for Christmas. I was glad that the next day, Friday the 26th, we were expecting a houseguest. He was our friend Tommy Hicks, a gifted evangelist, and a good person to have around when spirits were low.

"Because do you realize, Tommy," I said to him over dinner Friday night, "that tomorrow morning is the last meeting of the Full Gospel Business Men's Fellowship. ..." I grimaced a little. ... "International? It's pretty obvious everyone feels the same way about it — it's just that Miner was honest enough to say so. So the only thing to do is to terminate officially with some kind of announcement. Maybe figure out how we can all work together next summer to sponsor a tent meeting."

I was trying to sound casual, but Tommy must have caught the turmoil in my heart, because he said, "Demos, I think we should keep talking about this."

So we did, lingering on at the table, recalling for him our hopes and disappointments. After a while Gerry went to bed — Steve had been asleep long since, and Richard was leading a youth retreat that weekend. But Tommy, Rose, and I stayed on, talking about the various men who had come to Clifton's Cafeteria, remembering the things they had shared with the group.

"Never a Saturday I didn't learn something," I told Tommy. "Something that helped me love God better, and people better."

It was almost midnight when Rose looked at her watch. "Look at the time, Demos! And I haven't even cleared the table! We've got to get to bed, or we won't get to Clifton's ourselves in the morning."

"You go on to bed, honey," I said. "This thing's got me too bothered to sleep." I'd been so sure, a year ago! "I'm going into the living room and get down on my knees until I hear from the Lord about this."

"Good man," said Tommy. "I'll give Rose a hand with the dishes, and then I'll go to my room and back you up. But basically, Demos, this is between you and God."

Tommy and Rose carried a stack of dishes out to the kitchen. I crossed the little front vestibule and was stepping into the living room – when it happened.

Exactly as when I was thirteen years old, the air around me suddenly became heavy, overwhelming, forcing me to the floor. I fell to my knees, then on my face, stretched full length on the patterned red rug.

I could not have stood up, any more than I could have in my bedroom in the big Spanish house next door, twenty-seven years ago. So I did not try. I simply relaxed in His irresistible love, feeling His Spirit pulse through the room in endless torrents of power. Time ceased. Place disappeared. And as I lay there, praising Him now in English, now in tongues, I heard His voice, speaking the very words He had so long ago:

Demos, will you ever doubt My power?

And suddenly I saw myself as I must have looked to Him these past months: struggling and straining, a very busy ant scurrying here and there, dashing off to Europe to try to get the backing of an "official" group, depending everywhere on my own energy instead of His.

With a pang I recalled Oral Roberts's prayer at the very first meeting of the Fellowship, the prayer that had brought twenty-one people to their feet and set us marching to a hymn of victory. "Let this Fellowship grow in Your strength alone. . . ."

But I had acted as though it were *my* strength which counted – as though I personally had to start the thousand chapters that Oral had seen. And of course I hadn't been able to start a single one.

"Lord Jesus, forgive me!"

Next He reminded me of what I had seen in Europe – seen but not understood: the steel doors of the bomb shelter in Hamburg; the cinder embedded in my eye at the Grand Hotel in Venice.

I am the One, Demos, who alone can open doors. I am the One who removes the beam from unseeing eyes.

"I understand, Lord Jesus. And I thank You "

And now I will let you see, indeed.

With that the Lord allowed me to rise to my knees. Lifted me, almost, as though the power which had pressed me to the floor was now bearing me up. And at that moment, Rose came into the living room. She stepped around me and walked over to the Hammond organ in the corner. She said not a word, but sat down and began to play.

As the music swelled through the little room, the atmosphere grew brighter. To my amazement the ceiling of the room seemed to have disappeared. The cream-coloured plaster, the ceiling light – they were simply gone, and instead I found myself staring up into the sky, a daytime sky although outside it must have been pitch dark. How long she played while I gazed into that infinite distance I don't know. But all at once she stopped, fingers still resting on the keys, and began to pray aloud in tongues, a lovely, lilting, flowing message.

She paused a moment, then in the same lyric rhythm spoke in English:

My son, I knew you before you were born. I have guided you every step of the way. Now I am going to show you the purpose of your life.

It was the Spirit's gifts of tongues and interpretation, given together. And as she spoke a remarkable thing began to happen. Although I remained on my knees, I felt as if I were rising. Leaving my body. Moving up, away from the living room. Down below me I could see the rooftops of Downey. There were the San Bernardino mountains, and over there the coast of the Pacific. Now I was high above the earth, able to see the entire country from west to east.

But though I could see so far, I could also see people on the earth – millions and millions of them standing shoulder to shoulder. Then, just as a camera can zoom in at a football game to show first the stadium, then the players, then the very laces on the football, my vision seemed to move in on these millions of men. I could see tiny details of thousands and thousands of faces.

And what I saw terrified me. The faces were set, lifeless, miserable. Though the people stood so close together, shoulders touching, there was no real contact between them. They stared straight ahead, unblinking, unseeing. With a shudder of horror I realized that they were dead. . . .

Then the vision changed. Whether the world was turning, or whether I was travelling around it, I didn't know. But now beneath me was the continent of South America. Then on to Africa. Europe. Asia. Once more the startling close-ups occurred, and every where it was the same. Brown faces, black faces, white faces — every one rigid, wretched, each locked in his own private death.

"Lord!" I cried. "What's the matter with them! Lord, help them!"

Afterward Rose told me that I said nothing. But in the vision it seemed to me that I wept and pleaded aloud.

Suddenly Rose began to speak. Humanly speaking, of course, she had no way of knowing that I was seeing anything at all. But what she said was:

My son, what you see next is going to happen very soon.

The earth was turning — or I was moving around it — a second time. Below me again were millions upon millions of men. But what a difference! This time heads were raised. Eyes shone with joy. Hands were lifted towards heaven. These men who had been so isolated, each in his prison of self, were linked in a community of love and adoration. Asia, Africa, America — everywhere death had turned to life.

And then the vision was over. I felt myself returning to earth. Below me was Downey, California. There was our house. I could see myself, kneeling, and Rose seated at the organ. And then the familiar objects of the room closed around me, and I was aware of an ache in my knees, a stiffness in my neck. I got slowly to my feet and looked at my watch. It was 3:30 in the morning.

"What happened, Demos?" Rose asked. "Did you hear something from the Lord?"

"Honey, I not only *heard*, I *saw*." And I described the vision. Rose listened with tears glistening in her eyes:

"Oh, Demos, don't you see, He's showing us that the Fellowship is to go on!"

She got up from the organ and slipped her hand in mine. "Do you remember, Demos? It was in this room, nearly eight years ago, that we knelt down and put Him first. . . ."

As we started for our bedroom we saw a light beneath the

door of Richard's room where Tommy was staying. I knocked at the door and Tommy called out, "Come in!" He was prostrate on the floor, still dressed in his grey suit. He had promised back-up prayer, and he was giving it.

"Demos," he said, "tell me what you heard! Never in my life have I felt power like I felt tonight – wave after wave just pouring through this house."

We didn't get to bed at all that night. By the time I finished describing the vision to Tommy, it was time to drive downtown to Clifton's Cafeteria.

When we reached the upstairs room, two men were already there, waiting for us. One was Miner Arganbright – I was surprised to see him! The other was a fellow whose face was only vaguely familiar.

"I have something for you, Demos," said Miner. He reached into his pocket and drew out an envelope. His letter of resignation, no doubt. What a pity, just when I felt so –

But it was not a letter. It was a cheque. My eyes swept over the words: "Pay to the order of the Full Gospel Business Men's Fellowship International. . . ."

"A thousand dollars!" I said. "But, Miner, last week you didn't think the organisation was worth five cents."

"Last week was last week," Miner said. "Demos, I woke up early this morning and I heard a voice. It was God – I know it was God. He said, 'This work is to go around the world and you're to donate the first money.'"

I was still staring at him when the other fellow stepped up. "Mr. Shakarian," he said, "my name is Thomas Nickel. Something happened to me last night I think you'll be interested in."

I moved my tray next to his and salted my eggs while Mr. Nickel related that he too had received a message from the Lord in the middle of the night. He'd been working late at his printing press up in Watsonville, California, near San Francisco; because of Christmas falling in the middle of the week he'd gotten behind. Suddenly he heard the Holy Spirit clearly say to him, "Get in your car and drive to Los Angeles for the Saturday morning meeting of that group you've attended once."

He'd looked at his watch. It was midnight – the very hour, I recalled, when I'd gone into the living room to pray.

Nickel argued with the insistent voice inside him. Watson-ville is four hundred miles north of Los Angeles: he'd have to drive all night to make it. But the word kept coming: be at that meeting. Leaving a message at the Monte Vista Christian School where he was an instructor, he started south.

"And here I am," Nickel concluded, "to offer you my press and my services."

Rose, Miner and Tommy were listening intently too.

"Your press?" Tommy asked.

"To put out a magazine," Nickel said. "You see, what the Spirit kept telling me was: 'This Fellowship must go around the world.' But it's never going to get started without a voice. . . ."

"Voice . . ." Rose echoed. "Businessmen's voice. . . ."

The meeting that morning wasn't a very large one, but it was the most joyful one we'd ever had. Before it was over we had appointed Thomas R. Nickel editor and publisher of a new magazine to be called the *Full Gospel Business Men's Voice*.

"Just think," I said to Rose as we fell into bed that night, "last night at this time the Fellowship was finished. Now we have a thousand-dollar treasury and a magazine. I can't wait to see what the Lord will do next!"

9

Foot on the Table

The answer was not long in coming. Shortly after the New Year we had a phone call from Sioux Falls, South Dakota. It was Tommy Hicks phoning from the rear of an auditorium where he'd just spoken.

"Demos," he said, "I think you've got Chapter Number Two."

That evening he'd told the story of the Fellowship and the vision. At the end of his talk a man in the audience stood up and asked why they couldn't have a group like that in Sioux Falls.

"I told him, 'Sure you could.' I asked anyone who was interested to come down front, and Demos, it looked like the whole room came forward. You've got yourselves Group Number Two here in South Dakota."

It was only the beginning. Wherever Tommy went that year he talked about the Fellowship. He left a trail of enthusiastic men behind him and by the summer of 1953 we had nine chapters and were planning a National Convention in October — exactly two years from the first meeting in Clifton's Cafeteria.

Six hundred people showed up for that fall weekend at the Clark Hotel in Los Angeles. Today when a convention can draw twenty thousand, that first national meeting seems small indeed. But to us it was enormous — and so was the eagerness.

For instance there was the question of a budget. We had a full-time employee now, Floyd Highfield, who answered enquiries from men around the country, put them in touch with each other, and helped them get organised into chapters. One of these days Floyd was going to need a secretary. Then there was the magazine: Tom Nickel was donating his time and equipment, but someone had to print more than the five thousand copies a month we'd started with. We estimated that in 1954 we would need around ten thousand dollars.

So on the last night of the convention one of the speakers, Jack Coe, stood up and made the simplest appeal for money I have ever heard. Jack was a huge man with a knack for coming right to the point.

"We need ten thousand dollars," he said. "I would like one hundred men to come forward and pledge one hundred dollars each." Then he sat down.

At once men began converging on the speakers' table. Jack asked each one to write his name and address on a sheet of paper. At the end of the meeting we tallied up the names. Exactly one hundred men had made pledges. The budget had been raised to the penny.

And meanwhile, the Saturday meetings at Clifton's were becoming a different kind of problem. The first year we couldn't talk men into coming; now we couldn't keep them away.

The "upper room's" seating capacity was four hundred; we were squeezing in five or six hundred each week. Sometimes as many as seven hundred showed up, standing around the walls, jamming the staircase. For six weeks in a row the fire department sent officials, who threatened to close down the entire restaurant.

And so we held a meeting of the Board of Directors – still a little awed at finding ourselves with something to direct – to discuss the situation. We could find a bigger meeting place, the Clark ballroom, for example. Or we could encourage the men who'd been coming to Clifton's to start new chapters nearer their own homes. Long Beach, Glendale, Pasadena – why shouldn't each of them have its own "Clifton's," a centre of power from which the life of the Spirit could reach into the community?

I do not want a big centralised organisation. That was the message the Spirit seemed to give us.

Of course, come together on occasion to inspire and encourage each other, to light a fire bright enough for many to see.

But for your day-in, year-out work, I want you small, local, sensitive to Me. I do not want uniformity. I will never come to two men or two places in just the same way. Give Me outlets for My infinite variety.

And so the Saturday morning meeting at Clifton's became four groups, then five, then ten. Some met weekly, some biweekly, some once a month. Some continued to meet Saturday mornings, others chose a weekday evening. As these in turn got too large – more than three or four hundred men at a meeting – they, too, formed offshoot groups, until today there are forty-two chapters in the Los Angeles area, each with a flavour all its own. Some are demonstrative, some reserved; some stress teaching, others healing, evangelism, youth work.

But none would have existed without that first year of seemingly hopeless struggle. And so it was wherever this Fellowship spread – the first year in any area seemed to be the toughest.

Minneapolis, for example ... In 1955 a restaurant owner invited thirteen of us from the Fellowship to come there for the kickoff banquet of the first Minnesota chapter. We travelled through a snowstorm from all around the country. I flew with C. C. Ford, a builder from Denver, in his four-seater Cessna: I was grateful no one from our church could see us as the little single-engine plane bounced crazily through the sky.

Waiting for us at the Minneapolis airport was Clayton Sonmore. He made light of the storm. "We're used to snow here in Minneapolis. We'll have two hundred and fifty key business people out this evening."

At his restaurant we discovered why he was so confident of a big turnout. Fried chicken, homemade bread, fresh apple pie – waiters were already setting out the mouth-watering food on a long buffet table. All thirteen of us from the Fellowship had made it, I was relieved to see, in spite of the weather, and we stood around comparing notes on our journeys while Sonmore greeted the local men who were starting to arrive.

Seven o'clock arrived, the hour for the banquet to begin. Twenty-eight people had gathered in the dining room – thirteen of us – fifteen, counting Clayton Sonmore, from Minneapolis.

Seven-thirty. Twenty-eight hungry people eyed the laden buffet table. "The weather's keeping people home," someone suggested.

But through the windows we could hear a steady stream of traffic moving past on well-ploughed streets.

At eight o'clock twenty-eight of us sat down to eat, fewer people than there were tables in the big room. Sonmore's face was a study. I knew exactly how he felt. But I also knew something else. There was a pattern here. God's pattern. I told the discouraged restaurant man about our experience in Los Angeles – how we couldn't give breakfast away any more than he could give away dinner. "But God doesn't need vast numbers to launch His work. He needs only a few in each place. Don't look at the two hundred and thirty-six empty places," I told him. "Look at the fourteen men who came. With these fourteen, God can turn this city upside down."

It turned out to be a wonderful meeting. The main speaker was Henry Krause, a manufacturer from Hutchinson, Kansas, and chairman of the Fellowship's Board of Directors. Henry stood up and faced the nearly empty room as eagerly as though it had been packed. He didn't preach a sermon. Like all our men, he simply told his own story: how one day as he was ploughing his wheat field – and praying, as he often did alone on his tractor – God showed him a new kind of plough.

Henry Krause wasn't an especially mechanically minded person, but there was this machine before his eyes, complete in every detail. When he got back to the house he drew a picture of it. And the more he looked at it, the more he realised that with a plough like that – if it worked – he could plough three times as much ground with the same tractor in the same length of time.

Henry made more exact drawings and began taking them around to manufacturers. Everywhere the reaction of the technical experts was the same: the thing wouldn't work.

Henry was no expert and no technician. But he believed his design had come from God, and he knew that God was expert and master-craftsman both.

And so out in his barn Henry began building the plough himself, hammering it out blade by blade from scrap metal and secondhand parts. It took many months, working over a home-made forge, before the plough was completed just as he had seen it. He hooked it to his tractor and drove it into the field.

And it did work.

The Krause Plough was now used all over the world, and Henry Krause was one of the country's largest manufacturers of farm equipment — a businessman who devoted half his time and all of his heart to God's service.

An electric energy had built in the room. When Henry spoke you could literally *feel* the Spirit fall on a meeting. Three of the men from Minneapolis received the Baptism sitting at their table — without anyone laying hands on them or saying a single prayer. We were all gathered around them rejoicing, when a waiter burst through the door from the kitchen.

"Mr. Sonmore! Can you come right away?"

Down in the basement, it seemed, one of the maintenance men had had some kind of seizure. The waiter didn't know whether it was a heart attack or an epileptic fit.

Several of us hurried down the stairs. Outside the furnace room a group of men were holding another fellow in a chair.

And suddenly I began to laugh. This man wasn't sick. He was quite simply what the old-timers in the Armenian Church called "under conviction."

"Brother," I said, "praise God! Thank Him that He's sought you and found you tonight!"

The man opened his eyes. He looked scared to death — and no wonder. It must have been something to feel the power of God sweep without warning through that cement corridor. The man hadn't even known that there was a prayer meeting going on up in the restaurant.

Well, he came back upstairs with us, and you've never seen a more thoroughly converted individual. First he had a lot of things in his life he wanted to confess, then he couldn't tell God enough how much he loved Him.

The episode was like God's verdict on a meeting that by human measurements had failed. It was as though He told us, *Don't worry about numbers. I'll find the people I want, wherever they are, and I'll bring them to you. Do your part faithfully, and leave the rest to Me.*

And that's what they did, there in Minneapolis. That original little group of men — including one boiler-room mechanic — kept meeting steadily and regularly, seeing no growth for six months, no visible impact of what they were doing. And then all at once men started coming. Two hundred. Five hundred. A thousand — it was Los Angeles all over again.

So alive was the Minneapolis area, in fact, that a year and a half after that snowy night we held our annual nationwide convention there. And it was at that convention, in the fall of '56, that we saw the first real breakdown of barriers between Pentecostals and a mainline denominational church.

For years, of course, individuals of all denominations had been coming into the fullness of the Spirit. And in general they had faced two choices: to stay in their church and keep quiet about this new dimension, or to leave and join some Pentecostal group. But Pentecost welcomed and nurtured in the historic churches themselves?

We saw them the first day of the convention, sitting in the back row of the ballroom at the Leamington Hotel, as though prepared to bolt at any instant — five Lutheran ministers. Whatever they heard it was evidently not too alarming, because they were back the next night, and sitting a little farther front. The third day, a Wednesday breakfast meeting, they were there again eager to receive, they told us, "whatever Christ has for us."

A group of us from the Fellowship went to their table and prayed that Jesus would fill them with His Spirit. Afterward they thanked us courteously and left. It was all very quiet, very sedate and Lutheran, and we didn't know until later if our prayer had been answered.

It had been. One clergyman had received the Baptism while driving home in his car. Another while shaving the next morning. A third remembered one of the convention speakers saying that it is not when we strain and strive that we receive God's gifts, but when we are most relaxed. "Where do I relax best?" the minister asked himself. A moment later he was standing under a warm shower, praising God in a heavenly language.

It was the beginning of a transformation which has since swept Lutheran congregations from coast to coast. Not a rejection of their traditional strengths but the very opposite: an empowering of Lutherans, clergy and laymen alike, to make the statements of their faith a day-by-day reality.

Since then we've watched the same power sweep many denominations – Presbyterians, Baptists, Methodists, Roman Catholics, Episcopalians. Always at first a handful of half-hostile people coming to a meeting out of curiosity. Then the wind of the Spirit blowing through whole churches, whole communions.

It was only seven students from Notre Dame who spoke in tongues that Monday night in March, 1967, in the home of Ray Bullard, president of our South Bend Fellowship chapter. But the joy and power they found in that basement room were such that today Ray is regarded by many as a kind of spiritual godfather to the worldwide Catholic Pentecostal movement springing from Notre Dame.

The key again was the small local chapter, meeting regularly, sometimes in discouragement, praying for South Bend, waiting, as St. Gregory waited, for God's perfect time.

No man of course can see the timetable whole – only fragments here and there. In October 1974 a fragment was supplied for me when I was invited to the Vatican to receive an official appreciation for the role of the Fellowship in reaching "millions" of Roman Catholic laymen.

Millions? I thought dazedly as I walked out past the colourful row of Swiss guardsmen. *Millions. . . .?*

Don't worry about numbers. That had been God's word to

us from the beginning. *When the Spirit is in control, the numbers will be greater than any man will ever know.*

And when the Spirit is not. . . .

It was in 1957 that C. C. Ford flew me on a two-week visit to a dozen chapters through the South. We were especially impressed with the group in Houston, Texas; over six hundred turned out for a Saturday breakfast meeting.

"I don't know," one man said dejectedly as a few of us sat around talking afterwards. "We should be reaching thousands, not just hundreds."

"But you've only been going a few months," I said. "It takes time to. . . ."

"Not in Texas! In Texas we do things big and we do them in a hurry." He jumped to his feet. A lean, rangy real-estate salesman, his own career was perfect proof of his words. "Let's rent a hall! Hire a sound truck. Go out on all the radio stations. Get this town on its feet!"

Andy SoRelle, president of the chapter, shook his head doubtfully, but the other man took no notice. "We'll rent City Auditorium! Seats sixty-six hundred. When people hear Demos Shakarian's in town we'll pack the place out!"

I looked up at him in horror. "Me? Who would want to hear me? I'm no speaker. Besides I've got to get back for the hay buying and. . . ."

But the fellow would hear no arguments. C. C. and I would be travelling another week visiting chapters in Louisiana and Mississippi. "Come back through Houston. A week is plenty of time to get the word out, in Texas."

And because the man's love of God was also Texas-sized, I let myself be convinced. Or almost. All through the next ten days I forced down the knowledge that the big Houston rally was wrong. If there was one thing I had learned in the six years of the Fellowship, it was that in this mysterious reality called the Body of Christ, each individual had his special function. Some men were born organisers. Some were anointed speakers. Others could counsel. And when anyone assumed a function that wasn't his, he not only did a second-rate job, be blocked the flow of power to the person it did belong to.

As for my job – I'd been sure of it ever since trumpets rang out in the Hollywood hills. I was a *helper*. My gift was to provide a place and a time and a way for other men to shine. It wasn't a lesser gift than anyone else's, or a greater. It was simply mine.

But my name in lights over an auditorium? A meeting focused on me? It was wrong, and the more I struggled to prepare my speech, the more wrong I knew it was.

"What's the problem?" C. C. would ask as page after crumpled page of notes landed in the wastebasket. "You've given hundreds of speeches."

But that wasn't true. I never gave speeches. I stood up and – I don't know – *talked*. As long as I was doing what I'd been called to do, introduce other men, show people what their own possibilities were, the words were there. But at the thought of thousands of faces turned to me for leadership, my mind had gone blank.

By the time we got back to Houston I was in a state verging on panic. Andy and Maxine SoRelle had invited us to their home for dinner beforehand, but I was too worked up to eat. Even at the risk of offending their cook, Lottie Jefferson, I only stabbed at my food.

Around six forty-five we set out for City Auditorium in two cars: Lottie Jefferson, Andy – Maxine couldn't come – C. C. and me, and three other dinner guests. From a mile away we could see the lights of the place, glowing like the fires of judgment. Uniformed parking attendants sprang to open our car doors.

In the vast parking lot there were exactly five other automobiles.

We looked at our watches: 7:15. The rally was scheduled to start at 7:30. We walked through a side door into the big auditorium, eerily bright and silent — no one inside but a custodian way in the rear. "I got the spots fixed the way you wanted them!" he shouted, catching sight of the real-estate broker. We walked slowly down the centre aisle, footsteps echoing in the cavernous hall. The five cars must belong to the custodian and the lot attendants.

There was a row of chairs on the spotlit stage, but nobody felt like going up there. We filed into seven seats near the front — we didn't fill half of one row — and I looked at my watch again: 7:25.

And now a wild ecstatic hope began to fill me. Maybe no one would come! No one at all! Maybe God was simply stepping in to protect me from my own disobedience.

"I'm sure I got the date right in the papers," the real-estate fellow kept saying.

At 7:30 he, too, began to pray that nobody at all would show up. What would we say to them, how explain the "mammoth rally" where nobody came?

By eight o'clock it was clear that God had done the impossible. In a city where six hundred men could turn out early on a Saturday morning, He had simply drawn a veil of invisibility over a meeting that lacked His blessing. The real-estate man — with a heart as big as Texas — was the first to say it out loud and to praise God for it.

"But now what do we do?" asked Andy. "We've rented this big place for the evening. Shall we have a meeting anyhow, just the seven of us?"

"You've got something written out, Demos," said C. C. But nothing could have dragged from my pocket those much scratched-out pages.

"Well, then, I'll give the talk!" It was Lottie Jefferson. "I've always wanted to speak in a beautiful place like this!"

She got out of her seat, stepped to the front of the auditorium, and began to speak. She was a tiny little person, couldn't have weighed more than a hundred pounds, but when she talked about Jesus her voice filled that 6,600-seat arena. For thirty-five minutes she preached as though every seat in that place had been filled. And so full of God's love and truth was every word, that I felt all the tensions of the past week drain from me.

The only thing I didn't understand was the altar call she gave at the end. Because, of course, the six of us in her audience had all long ago "given our hearts to Jesus" as she was asking us to do.

Still, it had been a wonderful talk, one I would never forget. I heard footsteps. Down the long empty aisle came the custodian, tears streaming down his face, to kneel in front of the platform and give his heart to Jesus. And Lottie Jefferson, with the manner of an evangelist who every day receives hundreds into the Kingdom, put her hands on his head and began to pray with him.

Who knows? Maybe there hadn't been any mistake. Maybe the City Auditorium on that night was God's place for us after all, and this man the person He was seeking. I only knew that I'd been reminded once again — I wondered if other people needed repeating as often as I did — that it is only the Spirit who can draw men to Jesus.

And it is only the Spirit's gifts which He will use for this task. He had not given me the gift of evangelism. I was to be a witness, of course. Every Christian is. Only the place where I'd be talking about Jesus would more likely be a cow barn than a platform. That was the original dream God had given me after all:

An automobile salesman like Linwood Safford in Washington, D.C., talking about God to other auto dealers.

An attorney like Kermit Bradford in Atlanta, Georgia, telling other lawyers.

A dairyman talking to other cattle farmers.

It came so naturally that way, starting with a common language, a common interest. . . .

Like the interest every dairy farmer feels in cattle breeding. To us it's the most fascinating topic in the world: the search for that elusive perfect animal who will invariably pass his good qualities on to the next generation. Every month I'd pore over the journal of the Holstein-Frisian Association, studying genealogy tables. And each time I'd be impressed all over again by the Burke bloodline being developed at the Pabst farm up in Wisconsin.

I remember walking through those spotless calf barns for the very first time, looking for the little bull who would introduce this line into our herds. The first animal I stopped to admire was priced at $25,000 – many times more than I could pay. There were animals among these two- and three-month-olds selling for $50,000, others the same age going for $1,000.

And suddenly I saw him. In a pen along the south wall of the barn, a sturdy little fellow who stood out from the others as though a light had shone on him. It was the same phenomenon that never ceased to amaze me at meetings of the Fellowship, where in a roomful of four hundred people I would suddenly "see" the man I was to call on next. Now this two-hundred pound youngster stood out the same way.

I went over to his stall. His name was *Pabst Leader*, his price: $5,000. I read the particulars on him and liked what I saw: his dam was graded *E* (excellent milk production); his sire had already fathered over fifty *E* daughters. But these things were only confirmation of what I had known when I saw him.

"I'll take Pabst Leader," I said when the farm manager caught up with me.

Mr. Sylvester looked at me curiously. Breeders never made up their minds so quickly – only after extensive consultations with their advisers. "Are you sure? I wanted to show you some animals in the next barn, and Mr. Pabst thought you'd be interested in. . . ."

"Quite sure, Mr. Sylvester."

Well, he had the animal crated up and shipped out to us at an additional cost of $350 and I put down $5,350 against Leader's account. Generally a bull's first ten daughters give an accurate picture of what he will do. Every one of Leader's first ten inherited her father's superior qualities: appearance, disease resistance, the high quality milk production of his strain. Even some of our spindliest little cows produced offspring with none of their own shortcomings, all of his assets. Over the fifteen years that we bred him, he sired five thousand daughters, every one stamped with their father's unmistakable quality. Pabst Leader was that animal-in-a-million with the ability to pass on his own likeness every single time.

Meanwhile, Mr. Sylvester reported dolefully, an animal that had sold the same season for $50,000 had not proved a reliable sire. "He wasn't worth $5,000. And the little fellow you picked was worth double $50,000."

It was not an isolated experience. Every bull we bought from the Pabst farm proved to be a top investment. Witness? I couldn't help it.

I remember the day Mr. Sylvester leaned across the table in the farm dining room, very serious and solemn. "Come on now, Shakarian. You're not making these choices on the spot the way you pretend. You have an adviser, don't you? Someone who travels ahead of you and makes recommendations?"

"Well, Mr. Sylvester, as a matter of fact, yes, I do."

He glanced triumphantly around the table. "I knew it! Who is he? Come on! We won't raise the price on you because we know the one he's looking at."

"You mean you really don't know who my Adviser is?"

"No. Really! We get buyers and brokers through here by the dozen, all the time. Your man's obviously a pro."

"Knows more about animals than all of us in this room together."

"An old-timer, eh?"

"He's been in the business longer than anyone."

"Specialises in Holsteins does he?"

"Oh, absolutely."

Of course I kept it up as long as I could. By the time I gave them the name of my advance man I couldn't have had a more breathless audience. "The Lord Jesus *made* these animals," I told them. "You and I can only look at pedigrees. He sees what's inside an animal – and a man too."

It was the perfect opening into the hearts and minds of those men. The chance to show God alive in the world a man knows – that's what the Fellowship was all about.

The world a man knows – I thought of the time our chapter in Lancaster, Pennsylvania, was having such a hard time gaining acceptance in that conservative farming community. The chief objection seemed to be that the Fellowship came from "outside" – that our needs and problems were somehow different from theirs.

So one time when Rose and I were in Lancaster, the chapter invited several dozen local farmers to be their guests at dinner, and I stood up as a fellow farmer and tried to get them to join in the give and take.

Stony silence.

You know how it is: the worse you're doing, the worse you

make it. As my confidence grew smaller my gestures got larger. I opened both arms, then swept them toward me: "The Fellowship depends on the participation of all of us!" But the only thing my arms gathered in was the milk pitcher in the centre of the table.

It toppled over, sending milk streaming down the front of my best suit into my shoes. Too mortified to know what I was doing, I put one foot on the table and began to dry the shoe with the white tablecloth.

There was a gasp from Rose. "Demos! Whatever are you doing!"

And looking down at the table, I saw.

Hastily I lowered my foot. I felt my face flush scarlet and wished the rest of me could disappear beneath the table, too. "I guess I thought I was out in the barn for a minute there, folks," I apologised. "Any of you ever been milking a cow and suddenly had her kick the whole pail over on you?"

There was a chuckle from somewhere in the back of the room, then all at once an explosion of laughter. The room rocked with it for several minutes – and the meeting was transformed. Grizzled old farmers stood up and told how God had helped them through winter blizzards and summer droughts, and by the end of the evening the Lancaster chapter had a lot of new members.

"Do you know what changed our minds?" men said to me later. "It was when you put your foot on the table. We realized then that you really were a farmer, just like us. . . ."

10

The World Begins to Turn

In 1956 we chartered our first Canadian chapter up in Toronto, and from then on the word *International* in our title made more sense. Still, Canada and the USA are a pretty small slice of the world's surface. I kept thinking of the globe as I'd seen it turning before me that night in 1952. Millions of men on every continent looking upward, alive with love, waiting for the Coming of their Lord.

The decade of the fifties was almost over, and I couldn't see this happening. And then when the opportunity came – I almost missed it.

The invitation arrived in December 1959. Through CARE the Fellowship had sent aid to famine victims in the Republic of Haiti. Now came an invitation from President François Duvalier to hold three weeks of meetings in that country.

"From everything I know about Duvalier," I told the group at Clifton's Cafeteria that Saturday, "he's one of the most absolute dictators in the world." Torture, secret police – everyone there had heard a different story about "Papa Doc." "To go down there at the invitation of his government would be like saying we went along with all that."

It was Rose who challenged this. "In your vision, Demos, were any parts of the world left out because of the government they had?"

I tried to recall. No — every continent, every island had been packed with people, shoulder to shoulder, lifeless and hopeless the first time, joyously alive the second. "Political divisions didn't enter into it."

"Then I don't think they should enter into it now. The worse the political situation, the more people need to rely on the Spirit."

And of course, Rose was right. So it happened that in February 1960, twenty-five men from the Fellowship boarded a plane for Haiti. We didn't know that this first air-lift was setting the pattern for the next fifteen years. We only knew that each of us had somehow raised his plane fare, arranged to take his vacation in the winter — "and my wife was counting on a trip this summer!" — and come backed with the prayers of his home chapter.

The aircraft had barely taxied to a stop at the Port au Prince airport, when the forward door opened and in stepped a group of medalled and beribboned army officers. "Is Dr. Shakarian here?" said one of the group who was apparently the interpreter.

"I'm Demos Shakarian," I said. "But I'm just a dairy farmer, not. . . ."

"Welcome to Haiti, Dr. Shakarian. Your bags will be brought to the hotel. If you will come with us, please."

Before the stares of the other passengers we filed out of the plane and through a double column of soldiers at rigid attention. A rank of long black limousines was waiting for us. We never went near the customs hall for which we had filled out so many forms on the airplane. Under motorcycle escort we went screaming through town to the Riviera Hotel. There Senator Arthur Bonhomme, the senate majority leader, was waiting to meet us.

"Everything is ready for your meeting tonight," he told us in excellent English.

Discovering that I was a dairyman, he offered to take me on a tour of the local cattle market. I was fascinated by the people we passed on the way, some leading cows or a single goat, the women balancing tall baskets of pineapples, melons – even chickens – effortlessly on their heads. But to my astonishment, when we reached the market, the animals were being butchered and sold right there on the fly-swarming square. "It's the drought," Senator Bonhomme explained. "The worst I can remember. We're having to butcher because there's no grass for them to eat."

The Sylvio Cato Stadium in Port au Prince holds 23,000, and when our group of 25 arrived at 7:30 that evening it was nearly full. A large wooden stage 20 feet wide by 60 feet long had been set up for us in the centre of the playing field. I would have been just as happy without so many military uniforms on the platform with us, but Senator Bonhomme assured us that the presence of generals and government officials gave the meeting status in the eyes of the people.

We tried opening with some hymns, but soon found we had none in common. So we fell back on the staple of all Fellowship meetings – individuals telling their stories. Once again the businessman approach proved its value. Differences in theology, politics, race – they just never came up, as members of our group talked through interpreters about experiences common to all people – misunderstandings between friends, illness in a family, the struggle to make a living.

The following night every seat in the stadium was taken and thousands were sitting on the grass of the playing field. The third night Senator Bonhomme estimated the crowd at thirty-five thousand.

Not all of them, however, had come to pray.

The trouble started while Earl Prickett was speaking. Earl runs an industrial tank maintenance and pollution control business in New Jersey but the story he told that night was about his personal battle with alcohol. It should have been a good one for this audience; Senator Bonhomme had told us that alcoholism was a major problem on the island.

Earl described how he had started drinking with his customers because "you'll lose business if you don't." Earl, however, was one of those who can't stop. His wife left him, his doctor told him he was endangering his life, but he was powerless over the habit.

The noise in the stadium was growing until Earl was having trouble being heard. "At last both my liver and my kidneys were so badly damaged," he said, "that the doctor gave me six months to live." And at that point, he recalled, a friend had invited him to a breakfast meeting of the Fellowship in the Broadwood Hotel in Philadelphia. "That was the very hotel where the previous Wednesday night the bartender had told me to get out and never show my face in the place again."

I leaned forward, straining to hear over the growing uproar. I'd been at that breakfast meeting and I'd never forgotten Earl, in an immaculate white suit, stretched out on the floor begging God for mercy.

One of the interpreters bent down to me. "Do you see those men, Dr. Shakarian?"

I looked where he pointed and for the first time saw a file of red-robed, red-hooded men. There were perhaps three hundred of them, marching slowly around the cinder track that circled the playing field, a number of people in ordinary clothes following after them.

"Voodoo priests," the interpreter said. "They're trying to break up the meeting."

Now I could make out a strange staccato chant rising above the hubbub of the crowd. Hundreds were streaming from the grandstands to join the eerie procession.

The general at my right barked an order and the soldier standing behind him left the platform.

"What did he say?" I asked the interpreter.

"He's told the troops to stand by. They can deal with this."

"No! No, he mustn't!" I turned to the general. "Don't call in soldiers! Please!"

Through the interpreter the general explained. "If we don't stop them, I'll tell you what will happen. They'll keep circling till they've got a big enough crowd, then they'll start shouting. You won't have any more meeting tonight."

I looked to Senator Bonhomme for support, but he shrugged his shoulders: "I don't know what else we can do." I knew the senator was thinking not only of the people at the stadium but of the tens – maybe hundreds – of thousands listening by radio in villages and mountain crossroads all over the island. We'd seen some of these hamlets on a drive into the mountains that afternoon, a radio loudspeaker hung from a tree or a housefront, the only public entertainment through the long dark nights.

Earl was attempting to describe the miraculous change that had begun in his life that Saturday morning – the reconciliation with his wife, the medically "impossible" healing of his body – it was useless. He stopped talking and turned to me for instructions. The snake line following the hooded priests had a thousand or more people in it now, and was growing by the minute. And yet ... if we used Haiti's own strong-arm methods to protect the meeting, wouldn't we undo what we came for? We were here to demonstrate the power of the Lord, not the power of guns.

"Please, General," I begged. "Wait. There's a better way."

But as the twenty-five of us from the Fellowship gathered hastily at the rear of the platform, I wished I knew what it was. Before those thousands of people watching to see what we would do, we formed a circle, locked hands across shoulders, and began to pray.

After a while I opened my eyes and stole a look at the stadium. The situation was getting worse. Now there must have been two thousand marchers, and they were beginning to clap. The thinned-out crowd in the seats began to clap too, swaying back and forth in an ugly, pulsing way. The shouting started.

"I'm going to have to stop them," the general said.

"No," I said. "Not yet."

I bowed my head again. "Lord, this is Your hour! Lord, save Your meeting!"

From somewhere in the stands behind us came a scream. I whirled around, certain someone had been knifed. Soldiers ran across the field toward the sound. Then all of us saw a man and a woman, the man carrying a child in his arms, hurrying across the grass toward the platform.

On the other side of the field the march was turning into a rhythmic dance. The couple reached the platform. And suddenly Senator Bonhomme strode to the rear of the stage and stooped down above them.

In another minute he was back, holding in his arms a slender boy of maybe eight or nine who stared dazedly out of deep-sunk brown eyes.

"This boy!" he said. "I know him! He's from my district — I've known his family all my life!"

He looked from one of us to the other, literally shaking in his excitement. "He can see! It was while you were speaking," he said to Earl. "His eyes were opened! He can see!"

I still didn't understand. "You mean . . . he was blind?" I said.

The senator turned to me in exasperation. "*Born* blind!" he said. "Blind all his life — until this moment!"

Still holding the lad in his arms he almost ran with him to

the microphone. At first he could not make himself heard above the din of chanting and clapping. But gradually, seeing the tall, familiar figure of the senator standing at the microphone with a child, some of the people quietened down. The interpreter was apparently too stunned by what had happened to translate for us a single word of what the senator was saying to the crowd. But before long we all sensed a change in the mood of the stadium. Although the marching continued, the noise was definitely dying down. The clapping grew more scattered. All eyes were now riveted on the senator.

An electric reaction was sweeping the stands. People had begun to weep; here and there I saw hands raised to heaven. At last even the red-robed priests stopped their chanting and stood about in confusion.

The little boy who was the centre of all the thanksgiving was peering solemnly about him, struggling a little in the senator's grip. What he made of his first look at the world I couldn't tell, but it was obvious that he was seeing, for his eyes rested first on one object then another, returning especially to the bright ribbons on the generals' uniforms. Every so often he would look up at the stadium lights above us, staring straight into them until the brilliance made him wince and whimper.

His parents had climbed the stairs at the side of the platform and were standing now beside the senator. He turned and set the boy down between them.

But I continued to stare out at that throng of worshipping people. Shoulder to shoulder, heads raised in adoration — where had I seen such a thing before? And then of course, I remembered. . . .

When the senator stepped away from the microphone we asked the interpreter to take his place and make a simple altar call: Would all who wanted to know this loving Jesus, come down onto the field.

Out of their seats they began to pour, hundreds upon hundreds. Many who had joined in the voodoo march also hurried to the centre of the field. Soon the crowd spread from the foot of the platform in every direction. In twenty minutes five thousand people were gathered there.

The next day the stadium was packed by midafternoon; again thousands flocked onto the field when the call was given. There were more healings, some before our eyes on the platform, others elsewhere in the vast arena. The third night after the blind child was healed we estimated that ten thousand people responded to the invitation to know Jesus.

Many who could get close enough to the platform wept out confessions of sin, especially in the area of witchcraft and demon worship. All kinds of things were handed forward to the stage and left there. Balls of hair, bits of carved wood, little sacks containing bones and feathers. The sight that gladdened me most in the ugly heap were hundreds of red hooded robes.

The next-to-last meeting was over. I stood at the window in my hotel room looking out at the moonlit bay, too exhausted and too exhilarated to go to bed. Exhilarated . . . and worried. What had really happened at the meetings? A kind of mass hysteria? A mob reaction that could respond to voodoo chanting one minute, Christian evangelism the next, and could just as easily swing back the other way? What could these thousands know, after three weeks of meetings, of the reality of Christ? What would become of them now?

I knew, in theory, that we would be leaving them in the all-powerful hands of God. But in fact my faith was not strong enough to believe that this was enough.

"Show me that it's real, Lord. Show me that something really happened."

I noticed him clear across the terrace next morning. We were having breakfast on the broad outdoor veranda of the Riviera; our group from the Fellowship, Senator Bonhomme, and other government officials, a number of military men — the same group who'd been meeting every morning for breakfast and prayer. I was at a table with Senator Bonhomme and six other men when the waiter came smiling toward us.

"*Bonjour, messieurs!*" he said as he began to fill the coffee cups.

It was the first time we'd heard him speak. A glum-faced fellow, he'd served us each morning in total silence. When he reached Senator Bonhomme's side he spoke again, pressing his free hand over and over to his chest.

"He says," Senator Bonhomme said, turning to the rest of us, "that this morning when he woke up it was as if a heavy weight that had been pressing on him was gone."

He'd been at the meeting the previous night, the senator continued to translate; he had not walked forward, but while we were praying for those who had, he had said in his heart, "Jesus, if You are who these men say You are, I want to follow You."

Seeing all eyes on him, the man set down the coffee pot. The senator continued to translate: "All my life this weight has been there. Thoughts. Terrible, evil thoughts. I was afraid of myself, afraid to go to sleep for the thoughts which came."

The waiter was sobbing now. The senator interpreted his words: "This morning when I opened my eyes, the weight was gone. It was like I was made of light, like I could float right up off the bed. There was no heaviness inside me."

Someone else was crying. I turned to see a second waiter, tears streaming down his face, too. The senator translated: "I know this light! I also have had those thoughts. Four nights ago I came to the platform when they asked for those who wished new lives. Since then I have waited for the thoughts to come back, but they have not. My mind is the mind of a man and not a beast."

It was my turn now to dab at my eyes as I whispered, "Lord Jesus, forgive me! Forgive me for doubting that You are strong enough!"

Later the same morning, word came that Dr. Duvalier would receive three of us at the presidential palace.

One of the glistening limousines had been sent to transport us. "An audience with the president usually lasts five minutes," said the official who met us at the gate. "I do not know when he will see you, but there is a room where you can wait."

Inside there were some fifty men sitting around a huge anteroom, many with attaché cases at their feet. We sat down prepared for a long wait, but to our surprise, the door to the president's office opened immediately and we were invited in. I don't know what I had expected a dictator to look like. Certainly not this stout little man with enormous round glasses, who rose from behind his desk to greet us. In fluent English he inquired if we had had a comfortable stay. We talked about the meetings, the huge turnouts, the hold of voodoo on the country.

The five minutes stretched to ten. Then twenty. Doctor Duvalier asked a number of questions about cattle raising and milk processing in the United States. At the end of half an hour, he looked at his watch. "I would like to continue this conversation," he said, "but there are many people waiting."

"Before we leave," I blurted out, "may we pray for your country and people, here in this office?"

All of us bowed our heads, Dr. Duvalier and his staff included. The three of us from the Fellowship prayed aloud, asking God's blessings on the thousands who had attended the meetings either in person or by radio, and on the new lives begun there. Then someone asked Dr. Duvalier if he had a special request he would like us to pray for.

"Rain," he said instantly. "Ask God to give us rain."

We glanced at each other a little unsurely, but again we bowed our heads. "Lord God, who has poured Your Spirit into thirsty hearts, send rain, we beseech You, on the thirsty land as well."

The final meeting, that evening, was the most poorly attended of the entire time.

The reason was simple enough.

Nobody wanted to come out in the downpour.

11

The Golden Chain

It was May 24, 1975; once again Rose and I were boarding a plane at Los Angeles International Airport.

No crowd this time to see us off – only Steve and his wife, Debra, who had driven us out. No worried group of Elders from the Armenian Church, no anxious faces. Why should there be! In the twenty-four years that had passed since our first airplane trip, Rose and I had flown well over two million miles.

Steve and I exchanged a few words about the television programme he'd be filming for the Fellowship in Portland, Oregon, while we were away. Rose gave Debbie a final hug. Then Rose and I walked through the boarding tube into the aircraft. We were flying that evening to Honolulu enroute to Auckland, where our sixteen New Zealand chapters were sponsoring a week-long event called "Jesus '75." At last report, so many thousands were coming that the Fellowship had had to rent a racetrack called Alexandra Park for the seven nights.

Dinner was served after takeoff, then Rose leaned her head against the window for her usual airplane siesta. It was a good opportunity for me to prepare the answer to the first question these thousands would ask: What is the Fellowship?

How should I answer a question like that? In terms of statistics? Well, these were interesting, certainly. I got out a pad and pencil and jotted down:

* Years in existence: 24
* Number of states having chapters: 50
* Number of countries having chapters: 52
* Total number of chapters: 1,650
* Average monthly attendance at all chapters: over half a million.
* Rate of growth: one new chapter every day.

I smiled remembering Oral Roberts's Dream-of-a-Thousand-Chapters that had once seemed so impossible. Soon we'd have double that number. I went on writing:

* Monthly circulation of *Voice* magazine: 800,000
* TV stations carrying our "Good News" program: 150
* Weekly viewing audience: four million.
* Airlifts: three a year since 1965.

I put my pencil down on the tray. Was this really the way to describe the Fellowship? Counting heads, listing events? That wasn't it.

Well, then, what about our various ministries?

Healing, for one. We'd never put much emphasis on healing at the Fellowship, because right away it tended to get all the attention. But healings take place, just the same. All the time. Sometimes we'll invite a man with the Holy Spirit's gift of healing to conduct a special service. More often it will simply be an ordinary member going about his ordinary business, used by God at a particular moment.

My gift, for example, was in helping, not healing. And yet. . . .

In May 1961 the Fellowship had sent a large delegation to

the World Pentecostal Conference, meeting that year in Jerusalem. What a thrill it was to stroll through places we'd known all our lives from the Bible. The Mount of Olives, the Beautiful Gate, the Pool of Siloam — we were almost sorry when it came time to go to the auditorium. Three thousand people were attending the conference, and it seemed to Rose and me that they'd all arrived in the vestibule at once, and were trying to squeeze at the same moment into the lecture hall. The conference was so popular that delegates had to wear a badge in order to be admitted.

We spotted our friend Jim Brown, the Fellowship's delegate from Parkesburg, Pennsylvania, and together we stood back waiting for the crowd to thin out.

"Dee-mos Shak-arr-ian?" The voice was a woman's, the accent Russian or Polish. I searched the room for who could be calling me.

"There she is!"

Jim pointed. They were making their way through the crowd toward us, a man and a woman. She was short and heavyset, maybe in her late fifties; the man was the most badly crippled human being I had ever seen. He was bent into the shape of a 7. He walked clutching a cane with both hands, his torso parallel to the floor.

"You were looking for me?" I asked the woman. I couldn't even see the man's face.

"Yes, Mr. Shak-arr-ian. This man, he needs help." She explained that she had found him living in a lean-to outside the city. He had asked her to help him get to the auditorium, because he had heard that Jesus was healing people there. When they learned that every seat was taken, someone suggested they talk to me.

My heart went out to the ragged little man. Both of them, the woman told us, were Jewish. I had only to think of the Jews in the Fellowship — men like David Rothschild, president of our Beverly Hills chapter — to know that God has a special love for His covenant people. But what could I do here? I had no special pull at the conference.

And then an idea occurred to me. Suppose I were to give this man my own credentials for the afternoon? Jim Brown was one of the speakers today, but I. . . . "Here," I said, unpinning my badge. "You wear this. It will get you in."

I knelt on the floor of the vestibule and bent back, trying to reach the little man's coat lapel. At last I got the badge pinned, and was about to stand up when I heard an unmistakable voice:

No, Demos, do not leave this man. You are to pray for his healing. Right here.

I was taken aback. Here? Now? With the vestibule full of high-powered Pentecostal leaders from all over the world? I glanced up at Jim Brown. Jim had had a lot more experience with healing than I had, and he. . . .

You, Demos. Right here.

So, still on my knees, I spoke in the man's ear. "Sir, would you let me pray for you right now?"

For an answer the little man rested his head on the top of his cane, and closed his eyes.

"Dear Jesus," I said, "we thank You that You made the lame leap for joy here on these very hills. Today, Lord, another lame man is coming to You — one of Your chosen ones."

Tears trickled over the gnarled knuckles and dropped onto the floor. A group was beginning to form around us.

"In the Name of Jesus Christ," I told him, "stand straight!"

I heard something snap.

At first I was afraid the fragile little man had broken something. But the groan that came from him as he raised head and back a few inches was of release and not pain. With such an effort that his throat muscles bulged, he straightened another inch. There was the crack again. Again he struggled as if wrestling with invisible chains. Taller still.

If anyone in the vestibule had been unaware of what was taking place, the woman's shrieks turned every head toward us. "A meeracle!" she kept crying. "It is a mee-racle!"

The little man straightened the final inch, and gazed triumphantly into my face. From all around us came a chorus of praise and thanksgiving in a dozen languages.

I, too, stood up. I reached out and took the man's walking stick. "In His strength only!" I said. And sure enough, shuffling a little at first, then bolder and firmer, he began to walk back and forth, spine straight, shoulders erect.

Instead of the talk he had planned that afternoon, Jim Brown told the story of what had happened in the vestibule. No problem for the couple now about getting in; seats were found for them and us, too, in the front row of the balcony. Every now and then as Jim spoke, the little man would leap from his chair.

"I'm the one!" he would cry. "I'm the one!"

And he would skip and dance and cavort up and down the aisle, until I was afraid he would go home crippled again by his own exertion.

Yes, I could tell that story in Alexandra Park — though I could not explain it now any more than I could at the time. Unlike men with the specific gift of healing, I had not sought the experience. I had not spent hours and days fasting and preparing myself. Nor did the strange power stay with me more than momentarily, though needy people came hurrying to me for the remainder of the conference.

The best I'd be able to tell the people in Auckland is that healing is one of the normal functions of the Body of Christ, and that any member of that Body may be called upon, at certain times, to perform it. When that call comes, the key seems to be obedience.

I glanced guiltily at Rose, snuggled beneath the airline blanket, remembering a certain night in Downey.

We'd gotten into bed; it was midnight – time to be turning out the lights. But for some reason Rose was restless. She kept getting up, walking to the window, coming back to sit on the side of the bed.

I was mystified; usually I'm the night owl, Rose the one who can't get to sleep fast enough. "What's the matter, honey?"

"I'm going to telephone Vivian Fuller."

"Vivian Fuller!" The Fullers lived in southern New Jersey. Herb Fuller was president of our Philadelphia chapter and I seemed to recall, the last time we were there, that his wife had been having eye trouble. But at this hour of the night. . . . "Rose, do you know what time it is in New Jersey? Three o'clock in the morning!"

Rose sighed. "I know," she said. And yes, she agreed, it would be better to wait till morning. But I have never seen the Spirit of God make a person so unsettled. Rose could not relax. It was up to brush her hair again, back to bed. Up to see that the stove was turned off, back once more. Up to be sure the doors were locked. "For goodness sake, honey," I said at last, "make the call before you wear a hole in the carpet."

Rose fairly jumped for the phone. I was surprised at how quickly the party at the other end answered.

Rose listened for a while, then turned to me. "Demos, get on the other phone!"

I went into the front room and picked up the extension.

"Vivian," Rose said, "repeat for Demos what you've just told me."

Not sounding the least bit sleepy or annoyed, Vivian Fuller told me that her eye condition had been diagnosed as advanced glaucoma, and that it was not responding to medical treatment. Knowing she was going blind, she had tried to face it courageously, spending hours training herself to walk through the house without bumping into furniture. But gradually fear and discouragement had got the best of her. This particular night the depression had been unbearable. She had lain awake feeling abandoned by God, abandoned by everyone. "Please God," she had prayed at last, "if You love me, show me by having someone telephone me. Right now in the middle of the night!"

For a while there was only the hum of the long distance wires.

"Vivian," said Rose, "God not only told me to call you. He told me something else. He told me you're going to be healed. Completely."

I hoped my gulp didn't carry all the way to New Jersey. But Rose talked on, reminding Vivian of all the wonderful signs of God's power we'd seen together in the Fellowship through the years. Afterwards the three of us prayed for Vivian's total healing, beginning at that moment. When we finished it was 1:30 A.M. in Downey, 4:30 in New Jersey.

Several days later Vivian called back. "I don't have anything really concrete to report," she said. "But an hour after we talked the other night, something seemed to go pop inside my head. I don't know any other way to put it. The next day I went to the specialist. All he would say was that there hadn't been any deterioration since the last visit."

A few weeks later there was a second call from Vivian. Not only had the deterioration stopped, but the eyes seemed to be getting better.

Months went by, and then we were all at the Statler Hilton in New York City for a regional convention. I shared with the crowded ballroom Vivian's story: how some of the finest doctors in the East had diagnosed her condition as irreversible glaucoma. "But now . . ."

Vivian walked up the steps to the microphone. She described the agonizing progress of the disease, how each day she would say to herself that perhaps this was the last time she would see Herb's face. Then she spoke about the lowest point of her depression when she lay in her bed at three in the morning praying that someone would phone. She told the story of Rose's call, of the subsequent visits to the specialist, and of his delighted announcement that her eyes had inexplicably begun to respond to the identical treatment he'd been using all along. "I praise God every day for my wonderful eyesight!"

And Rose's obedience continued to be used. Even as Vivian was speaking people began leaving their seats and coming forward to the platform, until twenty-six sufferers from glaucoma were standing on the stage. In an atmosphere charged with faith, the entire ballroom prayed for them. Six months later seven of these twenty-six attended the convention in Washington, D.C. We still don't know about the other nineteen, but every one of those seven had been completely healed.

At every convention similar experiences are recounted — and more amazing ones than these. Terminal cancer cured on the spot. A cardiac patient given a new heart (not a healed one, a *new* one with no trace of the plastic tubes and valves inserted earlier by surgery.) A young man dead of a bullet wound from a .38 pistol, sitting up in a Jacksonville hospital and calling for water after a Fellowship director prayed for him. Another man certified as dead by a doctor in South Africa, raised to life when a group from the Fellowship prayed, today triumphantly carrying his death certificate in his breast pocket. And in every case, it happened when someone was willing to be obedient, no matter how hopeless or ridiculous it appeared at the time.

Or . . . our ministry of outreach all over the world.

The figure that God had given a group of us in prayer last December — 1 billion, 250 million people to be reached in 1975 — seemed so astronomical as to be unreal. But then, the whole electronic age still seemed unreal to me, and it was electronics which, already now in August, was reaching this unheard-of multitude.

By now the Fellowship's radio program was going out weekly in twenty-one languages throughout Europe, South America, and Asia. At home our weekly half-hour TV series 'Good News' was entering its fourth year nationwide, with new outlets this year in Canada, Bermuda, Australia, and Japan.

And an important part of this picture was our son Steve, now our executive producer. Microphones, dials, tape footages seemed to come to him as naturally as they eluded me. I shuddered, remembering my first day before the cameras. The idea of the "Good News" show was that I'd get other men talking about their experiences. just as I did at Fellowship meetings. It sounded simple enough, and since studio time is so expensive we hoped to film the first thirteen half-hour programs in one week.

But when I stepped onto the sound stage, saw the cables, the cameras, the men holding stopwatches, I balked like a cow in front of a strange stall. The script directions baffled me. *Stand* here. *Sit* there. *Turn your head* now. When the hot lights went on at seven A.M. I began to sweat; by noon I looked as though we'd been filming in a bathtub.

Worst of all was the teleprompter with my lines showing up in a little box attached to the camera. I got words twisted, I turned sentences around, until the poor fellows I was interviewing were as flummoxed as I was. At the end of two weeks' filming, I'd lost twenty pounds and my enthusiasm for the entire project. In desperation I went to the producer of that original series, Dick Mann.

"Let's not use a script," I pleaded. "Let me just talk to people."

You couldn't do that on TV, Dick explained patiently. Time had to be calculated to the second, the camera crew had to know when certain shots were coming. And of course his expertise prevailed – until the prints came back. They showed a mechanical man with glazed eyes in a wooden face.

The next series we did amateur style. No script, no rehearsal, just prayer beforehand, prayer while we filmed, prayer after we finished. I forgot the mechanics of production and concentrated on the man I was with. All of us felt the change at once – the flow of God's Spirit into that studio. Cameras stopped jamming, people arrived on time, the four interviews in each half-hour segment formed a perfect balance. Dick Mann couldn't get over it: every time he gave me the one-minute-to-go sign, he told me, I would finish precisely sixty seconds later!

Even harder-to-explain things happened. One time we were filming in Puerto Rico, eighteen stories selected by the chapters there. It was a tight schedule because we had to do all our shooting by daylight – and it kept raining.

On the afternoon I was to interview a man who'd been healed of leprosy, there was a regular deluge. The camera crew covered their equipment with tarpaulins and we sat around watching the rain stream down. Rogelio Parilla arrived and I shook the stump of a hand he held out to me. At first I thought it was the joy in his eyes that made the day seem brighter; then I realized a shaft of sunlight had broken through the clouds. The crew snatched off the rain covers and Rogelio and the lady who had come to interpret for him stepped in front of the cameras.

Through Sally Olsen he described what it had been like to learn at age nine that he had leprosy. The physical agony of the disease was easier to bear than being taken from his family and shut away in an isolation camp. Up till then he had never even seen a leper; suddenly he was living among people whose very appearance terrified him. And worse was to come. Within a few years he was the most disfigured of them all, so covered with hideous sores that even the other lepers would not come near him, but made him eat his meals alone.

And then one day when he was twenty-two, a group of Christians visited the leper colony and for the first time he heard the message of Jesus. It transformed Rogelio from a miserable and hopeless individual into one filled with joy and love. By now the disease had eaten away his vocal chords; he began to ask God to give him back his voice so that he could tell others about the new life he had found.

Some time later he heard about a healing service to be held in the Pentecostal Church of nearby Rio Piedras. An indescribable hope began to build in him. He badgered authorities into giving him a rare pass to leave the camp, and he attended the service, sitting in the rear well away from the other worshippers.

When the healing line formed he again hung back, waiting until all the others were finished. And as he did, despair overwhelmed him. The healing was done, he saw, by the laying-on of hands. No man would be willing to touch a leper.

At last the altar rail was empty. Rogelio hurried forward and knelt down. Pastor Torres stepped up to him and placed both hands on his head. Then he put them on his face, his shoulders, his back; he put both arms around him and embraced him – and in that moment Rogelio knew that he was healed.

It was many weeks before the doctors could believe what their own tests showed: that Rogelio Parilla was no longer an active case. At last he was released and for the last twenty-five years had preached all over Puerto Rico. God had given him not only a beautiful speaking voice but a singing voice too. The musicians who had come with him stepped forward and with a lilting calypso rhythm Rogelio sang to the glory of God.

The last note died away, and the sun disappeared. Cameramen and musicians had barely time to get their equipment under cover before the downpour resumed in earnest.

We shared the experience at a meeting of the San Juan chapter that evening. "Wasn't that lull in the storm timed just perfectly for the filming?" Uncomprehending faces gazed back. Nowhere else in all San Juan, it seemed, had the rain let up, even for a minute. . . .

This is the way we'd done the TV program for three years now – no scripts, no rehearsals, relying only on the Spirit. The shows were not slick, but they had a quality of truth that touched people.

Each station gave a local phone number after the programme, so that people who wanted to take some new step as a result could get in touch with someone from a nearby chapter. I had the figures somewhere on the number of calls we were getting, nationwide. I fumbled beneath the seat in front of me for my briefcase.

Rose was awake now, looking curiously at the columns of numbers I had jotted down. "What's 'TV 13/3'?" she asked.

"Thirteen shows in three days," I said. "That's the standard time we allow for filming now, right? And we never have to retake any of it." I dug out the reports. "I'm trying to find out," I said, "how many people are phoning in after each programme."

"*I* think, Demos," said Rose after awhile, "that how *many* people isn't as interesting as what happens. One single man, and how it changes him."

One single man — but which of the thousands of stories to tell? I let my mind roam across the country from Puerto Rico westward. The East Coast. The Middle West. Across the mountains, all the way to California. And beyond — to the opposite end of the nation, in Hawaii. And I thought of Harold Shiraki.

Harold was the very first person to call our TV number in Honolulu after the programmes began to be shown there in September 1972. He had not intended to tune it in that Sunday morning. What Harold intended to do was something very different.

Harold had been born on a small coffee farm in Kona on the island of Hawaii, the sixth of sixteen children. In the best Japanese tradition he was taught to work hard, to consider others, to respect authority.

Harold's father had Parkinson's disease; when he became too ill to work, the older children left school to support the family. Because they worked extra hours each day in the blazing sun, Harold was able to continue his education, becoming the first in the family to graduate from high school.

From then on Harold worked to see that the younger children had the same opportunity. He got up each morning at four o'clock, dressed by kerosene lantern, walked many miles to whatever coffee farm was hiring. Only when all of his younger brothers and sisters finished high school, did he allow himself to marry and start a family of his own.

By now Harold had moved to Honolulu, working first as a stevedore on the docks, then as a clerk in a grocery store, at last going into business for himself. Harold's habits of hard work paid off. By the 1970s he had managed to set aside a considerable sum of money.

And then most of it was taken away from him. It was

done smoothly. Smilingly. By men he trusted. When he realized what had happened, the faith he had built his life on collapsed.

It had been faith in human effort and decency – not in God. Nominally Harold's family were Buddhists, but like many of the island people they actually believed in a variety of gods and spirits. One, Odaisan, was particularly influential with them. There was a small stone image of him in the Japanese temple in Kona which the family would consult on all decisions. When the god was in favour his image was easy to lift. When it could scarcely be budged, the answer was no.

Over the years Harold had become disillusioned with these traditional beliefs, as he saw the bondage in which they held his family. His elderly mother, now a widow, spent her life in terror of offending one spirit or another.

When he moved to Honolulu, Harold had joined the Episcopal church because it seemed to offer freedom from such fears. He had tried to talk his mother into becoming a Christian too, but she explained that – although Jesus was one of the gods she prayed to – His primary interest was in white people. Every picture of Him, she pointed out, showed Him with a beard – proof that He could not have much concern for orientals.

Now, with the loss of his money, Harold turned to his minister. The clergyman listened sympathetically, agreed that injustice had been done, but counselled against going to court. "These things happen all the time in business, and there's not a thing you and I can do about it. I'd try to forget it."

But that was the one thing, Harold found, he could not do. He stopped eating, stopped seeing his friends, sat alone in his living room with the shades pulled down, feeling the hatred grow inside him. Honesty, sacrifice, long hours – if all this got you nowhere, what was the point to life? Death was better. Dead people could sleep. Dead people weren't cheated and robbed.

Harold knew a friend who had a gun. But he was not going to die alone. Before he shot himself, he was going to shoot two other men. Three – if he could get to them all before he was stopped.

The idea grew until it became an obsession – until it became the only idea in his head. A Sunday. It would have to be a Sunday, because he would tell the friend that he wanted to go hunting. A Sunday in September, as soon as the hunting season opened. . . .

The Sunday Harold had chosen arrived. His wife again begged him to go to church – he had not been to a service since his talk with the minister. Harold only shook his head.

"At least turn on the television," she begged him. "Watch a ball game." His strange indifference to everything alarmed her.

Harold shook his head again – then glanced warily at his wife. She must never suspect what he was intending to do. Sure. Switch on the set. Look at a ball game until she stopped worrying and went to church. He glanced at his watch. 10:35. The afternoon games would have started, back on the mainland. He switched on Channel Four.

Two men were talking together. One was white, the other – he wasn't sure. Polynesian, probably. (I chuckled at the recollection; how many times I've praised God for this curious quality of the Armenian face. Jews think I'm Jewish, Arabs take me for Arab. In South America I'm addressed in Spanish; in the East I'm assumed to be Indian. And now in Honolulu I was being taken for Hawaiian!)

In his distracted state of mind Harold could not follow what the two men were saying. Still leaning forward in his chair as he'd been to turn on the set, he simply stared at their faces. They were the happiest-looking people he'd ever seen.

190

He tried to concentrate on the words, but his thoughts were in too great a turmoil. So he continued to stare. And as he did a strange peace settled over the closed and shaded room. Love. Harmony. Hope – almost as though these things were flowing out of the television set itself.

At the end of the programme, a telephone number was shown on the screen. Still sitting on the front of his chair cushion where he'd been from the moment the picture on his screen came into focus, Harold repeated the number to himself.

A few minutes later he was talking to Roy Hitchcock of our Honolulu chapter, hearing words too wonderful to believe. "Jesus knows all about your situation   Jesus is the answer . . . Jesus loves you."

Today Harold is a leader not only in his own Episcopal church but in Fellowship programmes all over the islands. He never got back his money, but he was helped at the Fellowship to lay down his burden of resentment and rage and come away a victorious person. He has not only made a fresh start himself, he's helped hundreds more to find their own new beginnings.

Among the very first was his eighty-one-year-old mother. Seeing the change in her son, she realised that here was a power greater than that of the spirits she'd been appeasing so long. She and other members of the family made a heap of the various images and shrines they had kept in their homes and burned them in the yard of a church. Harold's mother died in 1973, a serene and radiant Christian.

It was experiences like these that assured us that television had a role in the vision I had seen of all the world awaking to life.

So did the modern marvel of jet travel. I started listing the countries where our airlifts-of-good-news had taken us:

England, Sweden, Norway, France, Italy, Japan, the Philippines, Viet Nam, India – over fifty of them. In most, after the weeks of meetings and rallies, something more important was left behind: a local chapter – often several of them – as a continuing centre of laymen's activity.

In other countries, such as Finland, Estonia, Yugoslavia, we could only wonder and pray about the long-term effects. I thought of my first visit to a Communist country, and the resolve that had been born in me then.

It was in Cuba after Castro had come to power, and our little group was staying at the former Havana Hilton, now renamed the *Cuba Libre*. Castro had made the hotel his headquarters, and the place bristled with armed soldiers, but we never caught a glimpse of the leader himself. Then one morning around two A.M. as I was climbing into bed, I suddenly knew that if I were to get dressed and take the elevator down to the restaurant, I would come face to face with Fidel Castro. I'd had too much experience with the Spirit by now to question such inexplicable bits of knowledge, so as quietly as I could I got back into my clothes.

Rose opened her eyes. "Where are you going?"

"Downstairs to meet Castro."

Rose, too, was used to this kind of nudging from the Spirit. "That's nice," she said sleepily.

Down in the restaurant the only customers were a group of very young soldiers – fifteen- and sixteen-year-olds I guessed – sitting at the counter drinking orange juice. A few years earlier, the waiter told me, the place would have been jammed at this hour. "North Americans," he said wistfully. "From the casino." He gestured upward toward the now-deserted gambling rooms on the mezzanine. "They didn't care what they spent."

He wrote down my order for one dish of ice cream and went off to the kitchen with a sigh. When he came back with it, he lingered by the table, seeming glad of the chance to talk. Cuban Spanish was different from the Mexican variety I'd been raised on, but we had no trouble understanding each other.

"When Premier Castro comes in tonight," I said, "will you tell him I'm a dairyman from California, and I'd like to talk to him?"

"Tonight?" the waiter echoed. "He won't be here tonight! He never comes in this late."

I finished the ice cream. "Tonight he will."

The waiter stared at me. "Someone told you he was coming here?"

I thought about that a minute. "Yes," I agreed, "Someone told me."

The man shook his head. "Impossible," he said. "He never comes in after ten o'clock."

And sure enough, it began to seem that the waiter was right. Another five minutes passed. Ten. The young soldiers left. I picked up my check and went to the cash register. The cashier was counting out my change, when there was a clomping of booted feet in the corridor. Through the door came eighteen or twenty black-bearded men in olive-green uniforms, some carrying rifles, others American-made machine guns. In the centre of the group was Fidel Castro.

Castro sat at a table and ordered a steak while the body-guard stationed themselves around the room and – having no one else to look at – looked at me. I saw the waiter bend down and speak to Castro. He, too, looked at me for a moment, then with a finger he motioned me to join him.

I sat down at his right, conscious of gun muzzles following me across the room. Castro asked a number of questions about dairying in California, and seemed disappointed when I would not let him buy me a steak. "When I come to visit you," he said, "I will drink a gallon of milk."

All over the room the bearded men burst out laughing. To

my relief, the guns were lowered, several of them lit up cigarettes.

I had known the revolutionary leader only through his nonstop radio speeches; I was surprised to find him in person an attentive and careful listener. "And what brings you to Cuba?" he asked after a while.

I told him that a group of us had come here to get to know Cubans in our own fields of work, and tell them what the Holy Spirit was doing among people like themselves in other countries.

Again to my surprise, he seemed genuinely interested. He told me he'd once been in the hospital in Brownsville, Texas. "Every week there were two men on television. One was Billy Graham and the other was Oral Roberts. I thought these were honest men and what they said were honest things."

We had talked for thirty-five minutes, when a very angry, very drunk North American appeared at the table. "Don't you people ever answer letters?" he demanded. "I've been waiting three months to hear from this so-called government!"

I couldn't follow much of what he said, but I gathered he was owner of a nightclub which had been closed by the revolutionary government. I was amazed at the man's daring in that roomful of soldiers, but he was apparently too wrapped up in his own troubles to notice them. "Your people are losing money too," he said. "Don't forget that! I was bringing good business down here!"

Castro's face had turned almost as grey-green as his uniform. "Good business?" he said. "Is that what you call it? Gambling and prostitutes? Was that all you people cared about in this country?"

I tried to catch the clubowner's eye. Surely no one could be so drunk or so self-absorbed that he could miss the cry in that question. *Did you ever care? Did you ever know us?*

But the guy was past hearing. "Don't give me the big moral line!" he said. "Cubans were making plenty off it. Why every time. . . ."

Castro stood up, his dinner unfinished. He was halfway to the door the soldiers following him, when he turned around, came back, and held out his hand.

"I'm glad you came," he said. "I wish. . . ."

The greyness was still in his face, and he did not complete the sentence. In a minute they had all gone, the nightclub owner following after them, still complaining, and I was alone at the table. I looked at my watch. Five past three.

I wish. . . .

I wish more men from your country had come to Cuba to pray instead of to gamble?

What if they had, I wondered, as the elevator carried me back upstairs. What would the world be like today if the millions of travelling Americans had gone with God's love for the people they visited?

What if they went now. . . .

From that night on this became my plea, everywhere I met with the Fellowship. Go! Tell the good news! Travel for God. Help to offset another kind of traveller the world sees too often.

And our men *have* gone. Gone as people who have received from the faithfulness of other places and other centuries, and have come back to repay a little of our debt.

I thought of a September evening in Moscow in 1966, seven years after the visit to Cuba, when I was able to tell 2,200 people gathered in the Baptist church the story of the Russian Pentecostals crossing the mountains to Armenia in their covered wagons. Twenty-two hundred people rising from their seats, lifting their arms to heaven, weeping for joy, as the Spirit swept that meeting.

The following day I had the chance to record the same

story for Moscow radio: to thank the Russian people from the bottom of my heart for bringing us the unspeakable gift of God.

I lowered my seat back a few inches and closed my eyes. Men all over the earth waking from death to life — yes, that was the Fellowship.

And I had seen it in our living room in Downey. What else had the vision showed? Men coming alive not only to God but to one another. Men who had been isolated coming together, discovering one another. That, too, was the Fellowship.

At the opening session of conventions now we liked to ask for a show of hands: How many Episcopalians here tonight? How many Presbyterians? How many Baptists? The best part to me was not that we got a response to every question, but that each time hands were raised all over the room. Catholics sitting with Methodists, Quakers with Seventh Day Adventists, so that when the Spirit descended on the meeting the two men embracing each other in the seventeenth row might belong to churches which hadn't spoken for centuries.

Races coming together. Things are changing now, but back in the 'fifties segregation was still an issue in many parts of the country. I remembered preparing for a world convention in Atlanta. We had the ballroom rented at a downtown hotel — over a thousand rooms reserved for five nights — radio time lined up, registration forms printed — all the interlocking details involved in bringing a large group together.

And then, a month or so before the convention, the hotel discovered that we were expecting, as always, a number of black businessmen. Well, they were going to arrange so-called identical accommodations nearby. The meetings could be followed on closed-circuit TV in a "luxurious" lounge.

It took about a million phone calls to move that convention out to Denver. And there we noticed a curious thing. The black turnout was not only big, it was a lot bigger than we expected. Finally an Atlanta clothing store owner shed some light on it. "My friends have been asking me for months why I go to that white man's prayer breakfast. But when they heard what happened about the hotel – well, I had to rent a bus to bring along all the people who wanted to come out here with me." (In the summer of 1973, incidentally, we held a regional convention in Atlanta's Hyatt House, 1,500 people each night, black and white indistinguishably together.)

Generations coming together. Under the leadership of Richard and his beautiful wife Evangeline there was now a full youth programme at every convention: many times in a hotel corridor I'd pass a long-haired kid and a middle-aged man in a business suit weeping tears of reconciliation on each other's shoulders.

People of all backgrounds coming together. Blacks and whites meeting together in many of our one hundred South African chapters. Protestants and Catholics asking one another's pardon, embracing with joy, in our chapters in Belfast, Ireland.

People tearing down every wall that stands between us and others. I recalled one woman who literally had to have a wall between herself and the rest of the world before she could feel comfortable. Sarah Elias was a musician who'd studied piano at Julliard in New York and sung under Leopold Stokowski. A tall, imposing woman, Sarah didn't look like she had a problem in the world. So when she stipulated "single room" for a regional convention in Indianapolis, nobody dreamed that a tormenting life-long fear of rejection lay behind the request.

As it turned out, every bed in the Indianapolis hotel was needed to accommodate the crowd that wanted to attend that May weekend in 1972. "I'm sorry," the registrar in the lobby told her, "we've had to put you in a double." He checked his list. "The other lady is Sister Francis Clare, of the School Sisters of Notre Dame. I'm sure you'll enjoy being with her."

Sarah Elias was sure she wouldn't. Brought up by Holiness people in a small town in western Pennsylvania, she'd been taught to distrust nuns in general. But the real problem was a tragic childhood. From the time her father shot and killed her mother when she was a tiny girl, through the years in an orphanage, to the day she was disinherited by the family which had adopted her, she had learned that people will reject you. And so she in turn rejected people, shutting them out of her life, whenever she wasn't working literally keeping a wall between herself and the world.

No one, as I say, knew these things about her until, rushing up to the room when she believed it would be empty, she found the other woman there. And Sister Francis Clare, a wise and gentle Christian with a specific ministry in the healing of memories, asked if she might pray for Sarah. Out it all came, in the hours that followed, the fear, the resentment, the bitterness; in flowed the love and acceptance of God.

When I saw Sarah that evening her face was so transfigured that I asked her to come to the microphone and tell us all what had happened. Afterwards she sat down at the piano. When she finished that entire convention got to its feet and applauded until she played again. There were four standing ovations, and at the end all of us knew that the Spirit Himself had played for us that evening.

Sarah Elias was one of a whole category of people now served by the Fellowship. Business and professional women. In the beginning I'd been so concerned for the men who were missing out on life, that I hadn't been aware of anyone else. The women in the early years of the Fellowship – and there were many – were generally the wives of such men, Christians themselves, looking for a way to reach their husbands.

Then as the Fellowship got better known, a new group of women appeared. Married and unmarried, young and old, they were working people who — like men — felt left out of traditional church programmes. Sewing circles, rummage sales, morning coffees — they were as out of the question for these doctors, teachers, office workers, as they were for me. We had women lawyers attending now, actresses, factory workers. "*Salesladies*," I wrote on my paper. "*Nurses. Newspaper women.*"

"Demos?"

Rose was nudging me and I looked up to see the stewardess standing over us with a tray of sandwiches. We'd be in Honolulu in a little over an hour.

"*Stewardesses*," I added to the notes in front of me. There'd been five or six at the last convention. I re-read the handwritten pages. Outreach all over the world, in all kinds of ways, to all kinds of people. Did that portray the Fellowship?

What was it Rose had said? Tell about one individual and how he changed. It was true — all the statistics in the world couldn't convey the wonder of a single life reborn of the Spirit.

But where could I start? Or stop? The minute I told the fabulous story of George Otis, or Walter Black, or General Ralph Haines, I'd run out of time and have to leave out the equally fabulous story of Jim Watt, or Otto Kundert, or Don Locke.

There were a million stories now in the Fellowship, each one as wonderful as the next, each one unique, yet each linked to all the others in a golden chain.

Each one linked. . . .

Why not tell the story of one such link, one sequence in the endless chain reaction that is the Full Gospel Business Men's Fellowship . . . ?

199

It was a Friday morning in the early 'sixties when I received a telephone call from a young man who told me that we had met recently at a Fellowship convention in Oklahoma. "Mr. Shakarian," the young man said, "I wish you could talk to my uncle. I think he's ready to know the Lord."

"Who is your uncle?"

"Shannon Vandruff."

The name sounded vaguely familiar. "Where does he live?"

He gave me an address in a very swank area of Downey.

"What does he do?" I asked a little nervously.

"He's a builder. Have you ever heard of Cinderella Homes? That's his company,"

Well, my first thought was that I could never talk to *him!* Everybody out our way knew Cinderella Homes – it was a big, big business.

But at least I promised to give Shannon Vandruff a call, and the next day, Saturday, I did. Far from being a high-pressure type, Shannon proved easy and comfortable to talk with. And his nephew was right: Shannon was ready to hear the good news of Jesus. He and his wife, Veta, invited Rose and me that very evening to their large home by the golf course, later went with us to a Fellowship convention in Phoenix, Arizona, where both received the Baptism in the Holy Spirit.

Now a new name entered the chain reaction. Dr. Ray Charles Jarman was the pastor of the big church in South Gate, California, which the Vandruffs had attended for fourteen years. Under Dr. Jarman's brilliant preaching, it had grown into a million-dollar institution with upholstered seats, thick carpets, air conditioning, imported marble statuary. Dr. Jarman also had a daily radio programme and was a force in the intellectual life of Southern California.

The only thing the Vandruffs had never heard him preach was Christ. Like many a well-educated minister, he had long ago ceased to believe in the divinity of Jesus, miracles, and other "pre-scientific" concepts. But he was a conscientious pastor, who sincerely wanted to give his congregation something real.

And for fifty years he sought this elusive reality. He went into Religious Science, New Thought, Christian Unity, Christian Science. Finding his own life increasingly empty, he turned to Eastern religions, studying for three years under Paramahansa Yogananda, among others. He went on to Rosicrucianism, and after that to Theosophy.

In 1961, before the drug was declared illegal, he entered a clinic in San Francisco where he paid a nurse, a doctor and a psychiatrist to stay with him during a twenty-four-hour experiment with LSD. Far from providing a revelation of God, it gave him nightmares which recurred for months.

Meanwhile, after his own conversion, Shannon Vandruff had gone on a quiet campaign to get Jarman to a Fellowship meeting. The erudite minister was emphatically not interested. For nearly four years Shannon kept at him. Jarman got to the place where he hated to see the man coming.

At last a mutual friend invited Jarman to an evening of "Christian music and fellowship" at the Vandruffs'.

With a shrug, Dr. Jarman agreed. What did he have to lose? It would be another experiment.

Which is how it was that in August 1965 Ray Charles Jarman drove out to Shannon's with three people from his church. The Vandruffs' enormous living room was so crowded it was difficult to find a place to sit. Jarman noticed a radiance in these people which puzzled him – and annoyed him. If he hadn't brought people with him, he would have left right then.

As the evening went on, Jarman grew more and more uncomfortable. There was singing, prayer, testimony followed by exclamations of "Praise the Lord!" Jarman kept thinking of what his university friends would say.

Then about halfway through the evening the front door opened and there, supported by two men on either side of her, stood the most emaciated woman he had ever seen. Deep circles outlined her eyes, her clothes hung as though there were no body at all beneath them.

The woman was my sister Florence.

As Jarman watched in horror, the men half-carried her across the room and lowered her into a chair. It was twenty-five years since Florence's automobile accident. And what a quarter-century of service it had been! Often with Rose at the piano or organ, Florence had sung in churches and Fellowship meetings the length and breadth of the country. Now, precisely when the dream had foretold, she was dying – of a rare form of cancer.

"Florence Shakarian Lalaian," Shannon said, "do you have strength enough to sing for us?"

Florence smiled. "I'll try," she said. She put both hands on her own forehead and pushed it back, not having the strength to raise her head. Then she began to sing.

And Ray Jarman found himself face to face with the Reality that he had sought so long. Jarman was an opera buff; he had heard most of the great voices of our day. "But I had never heard a voice like this," he told me later. "When she sang it was as though an angel stood in the room." Florence asked them all to join in the chorus to "How Great Thou Art." As they did her voice soared above the others, higher and higher like a meadowlark, until Jarman felt he was standing at the gate of heaven.

It was Florence's last song. And for Ray Charles Jarman the first time in his life that he had wept in public.

But so ingrained was his habit of intellectualising everything, that his mind continued to resist what his spirit now knew. It was not until some months later that he took the terrifying step of jumping beyond where his understanding could take him. In his widower's apartment, with Shannon Vandruff as his witness, he got down on his knees – another thing he had never before done – and asked Jesus to take over his life. He stood up as fulfilled and joyous as he had once been empty and afraid.

It is this new Ray Jarman that hundreds of thousands of men have heard in Fellowship meetings around the world. "I preached for fifty-two years," he'll tell us, "before I knew Jesus." But who knows, in the last nine years, how many men Ray Jarman has reached, and how many of those, in turn, have reached others? Where does the golden chain end which links each of us to each other one?

Where does it begin?

I thought of the links forged before I was born. Magardich Mushegan prophesying back in Kara Kala: "A year from today you will have a son." Thought of that son driving a wagonload of vegetables behind a horse named Jack. What a strong link it was that joined the lives of the Shakarians and the Mushegans. It was Magardich's grandson, Harry, who one Sunday in 1955 received a vision in the Armenian Pentecostal Church on Goodrich Boulevard. He had seen the sanctuary filled with light and streams of oil pouring from heaven upon Isaac Shakarian. It was an ordination, the only kind our church recognised. And so for nearly ten years Dad had served as lay pastor of the church, receiving no salary, of course, in the Armenian tradition, obtaining a licence from the state to marry and bury, preaching each Sunday, caring for the needs of the people.

Then one Friday evening in the fall of 1964, Harry Mushegan had another vision. I was at the Coronado Hotel just south of San Diego that evening, November 6, at the start of a three-day regional convention. Our daughter, Gerry, and her husband, Gene Scalf, were there too; they loved the Fellowship, but with two small girls couldn't often be at the meetings. I knew how many arrangements they'd made so that both of them could attend this one, so I was surprised when Gerry came to me and said we must all go back at once to Downey.

"It's Grandfather," she said, "He's ... he's in the hospital."

"The hospital? But he's not sick! He was feeling fine when I left the office this afternoon!"

At the hospital reception desk they told me Dad was in the building across the street. It was strange, I thought, as I stepped into the small one-storey house, that they would put him here where it was so dark and deserted. Where were the nurses and – and then I realised that this little building was the morgue.

Dad was lying on a tall white table. It was no wonder that no one had been able to tell me. Never had a father and son been so close. I stood there in the bare little room hearing his voice, as I had hundreds of times over the years when an opportunity opened up somewhere in the world to tell men about Jesus: "You go, Demos. I'll take care of the business."

At home Dr. Donald Griggs was waiting for us. I had been right – Dad had not been sick. "He died the way the old patriarchs died," Dr. Griggs said. "In strength, not in sickness. He was reading the evening paper and he fell asleep."

No one but Dr. Griggs and the immediate family knew, so we were surprised when Harry Mushegan telephoned from Atlanta, Georgia, where he now had a pastorate.

"The old men!" he said. "I've just seen them all! My grandfather, my father, all the old men I remember as a boy. And some I never saw. About an hour ago I saw all these men with long white beards laughing and running and holding out their arms as though they were welcoming someone. And then I saw Isaac, running toward them."

There was a pause over the telephone. "Isaac is gone, isn't he?"

The seat belt sign was on for landing; the plane was banking, beginning its descent.

You go, Demos. . . .

That was what God said to each of us, wasn't it? *You go, Jim. John. Bill. Mary.* He didn't always tell us where, at the start of the journey. I thought of the second message the Boy Prophet received so long ago, still sealed and unopened. Does it foretell a great persecution coming to Christians in America, just before the Lord returns? Personally I think so. I think the Spirit is being given us in preparation for this time: to bind us into a Body, to assign to each one of us the task he alone can do for the welfare of that Body. I often wonder who will be told to open that message and read it to the church.

But that's not the important thing. The important thing is that He tells each of us to go. Go with whatever gift He has given — knowing that when we find that gift and use it, no matter what the condition of the world around us, we will be the happiest people on earth.

The plane touched down with a little bump and taxied toward the terminal. Rose rummaged under the seat for our things.

"You ready, Demos?" she said.

"I'm ready, Rose."

We stepped into the aisle and set out together toward the next adventure.

If you have enjoyed this book you will also enjoy . . .

Bill Bair
LOVE IS AN OPEN DOOR

'I want you to quit your job and start working with the kids I will bring to you.'

These are the words Bill Bair believed he heard at a church service. Bill had progressed in 18 years from a ditch digger to an executive position with the gas company. Could God really be asking him to do this?

The young people who come to Bill's door are problem kids – drop-outs, drug addicts, school failures.

'A poignant, memorable story . . . a heart-warming book.' – *Methodist Recorder*

Mary Wang
GOD'S SCHOOL IN RED CHINA

The First Medical College of Shanghai, with 2,000 students, was part of Chairman Mao's vision to put a doctor within reach of everyone, however remote, whatever his income. It was also Mao's ambition that each student should become a convinced communist. This is the story of an uncompromising group of Christians who continued to meet for prayer and Bible study in what Watchman Nee called 'a divine settlement planted in the midst of Satan's territory.'

Mary Wang was one of those teenage students. Today she is director of the Chinese Overseas Christian Mission.

'There is a golden simplicity and directness about Mary Wang.' – *Church Times*